All My Love, Kate

All My Love, Kate

Trudy J. Morgan

REVIEW AND HERALD PUBLISHING ASSOCIATION

Washington, DC 20039-0555

Hagerstown, MD 21740

Edited by Raymond H. Woolsey
Book Design by Richard Steadham
Cover Photo by Meylan Thoresen

Printed in U.S.A.

Library of Congress Cataloging in Publication Data

Morgan, Trudy J., 1965-
  All my love, Kate.

  1. Morgan, Trudy J., 1965-   . 2. Seventh-day
Adventists—Canada—Biography. 3. High school
students—Canada—Biography. I. Title.
BX6193.M675A32   1986   286.7'32'0924   [B]   85-24456
ISBN 0-8280-0318-1

DEDICATION

*To My Parents.
Without their love,
encouragement, and
constant reminders,
I would never ever
have met a deadline.*

CONTENTS

Add to your faith virtue;
And to virtue knowledge;
And to knowledge temperance;
And to temperance patience;
And to patience godliness;
And to godliness brotherly kindness;
And to brotherly kindness charity.
*   For if these things be in you, and*
abound, they make you that ye shall
neither be barren nor unfruitful in
the knowledge of our Lord Jesus Christ.
*   —2 Peter 1:5-7*

WEEK OF PRAYER
Faith Is for Real

Dear God,   October 14

It feels kind of strange to be writing to You. I guess it's kind of an experiment. But then, somehow, I feel like this whole thing is almost an experiment. That's not the way You meant it to be, is it? Still, I do have that feeling about it. As though, if it doesn't work out, I can always go back to the comfortable way things were before.

* * * * *

The washroom was crowded, as usual. Kate waited in the back of the lineup, standing on tiptoe so she could see above the heads of the others. That didn't work too well, though, because the mirrors were positioned so low that she couldn't see the top of her head. She sighed and resigned herself to waiting.

Betty Jane entered, high heels clicking. "Full of freshmen, as usual," she muttered to Kate in pretended disgust. They had attained the dignity of becoming seniors only a month before, and they were still very conscious of their superiority.

Betty Jane was not the type of girl to stand at the back of a lineup, Kate knew. She plowed her way through the crowd of girls, pulling Kate with her. "Honestly, I think we should petition for a separate bathroom for seniors. We need another washroom anyway. All of us have to go to chapel at the same time, and of course all of us have to comb our hair before we go

. . ." Betty Jane never seemed to stop talking. She chattered in an offhand way, never really seeming to expect an answer but just talking as though to fill up the silence. Kate figured that there were a lot of things one just had to accept in a friend, and Betty's chattering was one of those things.

Kate opened her purse and took out an elastic band. "Are you still torturing your hair like that?" Betty Jane wanted to know. "Those things will cut your hair right in half, you know that? Your mother is right. Leave it down." Betty Jane had had her long blonde hair cut short over the summer, and she no longer had to contend with hair falling over her face and into her eyes as Kate did.

Kate rolled her eyes and replied, "My mother doesn't understand what it is to be young today"—which she didn't really mean—and put her hair up in a ponytail. Mrs. Nichol was more understanding about the problems of youth than many parents, but she didn't approve of ponytails. Kate's hair went up every morning and came down every afternoon within the confines of the school washroom.

Betty Jane was already impatient. "You should get it cut," she said, and then dropped the subject. Together the two girls made their way to the chapel. The bell was already ringing.

There were two empty seats in the very last row on the girls' side, and Kate and Betty Jane slipped into them just as the chapel doors closed. "Narrowly missed another tardy," Kate whispered.

"I don't care," Betty Jane replied in her piercing stage whisper. "I still haven't figured out whether I'd rather be here or in algebra class!"

Kate smiled at what Betty Jane had intended for a joke, and signaled to her friend to be quiet. This was the fourth meeting of the fall Week of Prayer. Betty Jane was getting a little tired of daily sermons.

I don't think she really means it, though, Kate

thought. Betty Jane and I feel pretty much the same way about Week of Prayer and stuff like that, but it's part of her act to pretend it's all a tremendous bore. I enjoy the meetings, actually, if the speaker is good. It's just that they always make a big pitch for you to give your heart to the Lord, and I've done that so many times that it's no big deal.

Betty Jane subsided into silence as the program began. Kate stretched and savored again the luxury of sitting in the coveted back row. She looked pityingly at the freshmen in the very front row, right under the speaker's nose. It would take them four long years to move back, gradually, as she had done. The thought of it made her nostalgic for the three years of academy she'd already been through. This last year would be so short—and what then? One thing was for sure, life outside high school wasn't going to be anything like what she'd already known.

Kate looked from the freshmen to the speaker and then back to Betty Jane, who was doodling on a piece of scrap paper. She wondered how her academy years would have been different if she and Betty Jane had gone to boarding academy in their sophomore year, as they'd fought so valiantly to do. Betty Jane's parents had almost given in, but the Nichols were impossible to convince. Kate could still hear her mother's voice!

"We have a perfectly good day academy right here in town. You can get a Christian education and still be at home. Fifteen years is much too young for you to be away from home—and there's still a lot you need to learn here."

Well, Kate admitted grudgingly, they were right. There are some advantages to staying home after all. One up for parental wisdom.

She turned her attention back to the speaker, trying to gauge from his delivery whether or not he'd make a call today. She hoped not. She could already feel the familiar goosebumps, the churning in her stomach, the trembling of her knees as she rose to stand with the others. No matter how many times she sat through a Week of Prayer call, the feelings never changed.

Some of these kids, such as Nancy and Bob and Jean, would stand up with tears running down their cheeks and even go to counsel with the pastor afterward. For a week or so the spirit of reform would blow briskly through the school, and then everything would be back to normal. Bob would be secretly drinking out behind the grocery store at lunchtime, Nancy would be regaling the class with the latest in dirty jokes, Jean would get caught smoking in the janitor's closet again. Unless, of course, she'd figured out how to avoid getting caught.

And I'm just as bad as they are, Kate thought suddenly. The involuntary thought wouldn't go away, no matter how she tried to stifle it. Mentally, she shifted the blame.

These preachers work us up to a fever pitch of excitement during Week of Prayer, she told herself, and when they leave, life goes back to normal, things calm down, and everybody forgets all the promises made. All these kids get is an emotional high and then it doesn't make any difference to them. That's not real Christianity at all.

Having forgotten that she'd started out by condemning herself, Kate settled back comfortably and listened to the rest of the message.

The dismissal bell rang while the speaker was still preaching. Kate could tell that he was trying to wrap it up quickly as the students grew steadily more restless, the noise starting from the seniors at the back and building in momentum as it reached the freshmen in front. People started collecting their books and putting on their jackets. A momentary calm descended as the speaker prayed, and then, as if the "Amen" had released a cork from a bottle, the noise gushed out and flowed over the whole auditorium as the students filed out.

Kate and Betty Jane headed for the lab. "Another exciting chem lecture," Betty Jane announced. Kate left her books on the desk and headed out to the bulletin board to check the announcements.

"Afraid you might have missed one of our exciting school events?" Anne Reynolds asked. Kate grinned. "No, I'm waiting for them to announce that I've won the beauty pageant." She was used to being teased about her habit of reading every announcement that was posted. She wasn't looking for anything in particular—she just hated to miss anything.

Notices about the change in class schedules for Week of Prayer dominated the bulletin board. The only other notice posted also had to do with Week of Prayer—a listing of the times when Pastor Walters would be available for counseling. Thursday, 11:00-12:30.

Kate wondered what she would talk about if she went to see the pastor. Usually one of the repentant trouble-makers asked Kate to go along with her, and Kate had to get the conversation started. Some kids went just to get out of classes, but most were too shy about talking to the pastor to try that. The kids who went for counseling were mostly those who cried when calls were made and promised to give up their wicked ways—for a week at least. None of the "good" kids went, unless they had to accompany someone, or maybe their parents knew the visiting pastor and had asked them to pass along greetings and invitations. Kate had never gone to talk with one of the pastors by herself.

And I'm not going now, she assured herself, and was immediately surprised that she had even thought about it. Unless maybe I could tell him how pointless Week of Prayer is, how none of those kids ever really change. I'd ask him what we could do to make it last. But why should he care? He'll be gone by Sunday morning and he'll never see any of us again.

The bell sliced through her thoughts, and she raced down the corridor toward the lab. On the way she collided with Terry Fields.

"Watch where you're going! The building isn't on fire!"

"No," Kate called over her shoulder as she hurried on, "but I'll disappear in a puff of smoke if I'm late for one more chemistry class!"

"Good luck!" Terry called. Everybody in the school was familiar with the wrath of Mr. Hanson toward latecomers—and Kate was widely known to be the worst offender.

She had planned to rush in breathlessly and slide into her seat, but as she approached the closed door she realized that she'd need a good running start for that. Bumping into Terry had slowed her down. She opened the door quietly, slipped inside, and tiptoed to her desk. Mr. Hanson turned from the board and shook his head in affectionate dismay. "After class, Kate," he said. "As usual." He continued with the lesson.

Just my luck, Kate thought. She had needed that break between chem and English to finish her English composition from last night—but now she would be spending it listening to Mr. Hanson's lecture. He still felt he had to reprimand her for lateness, but deep down, Kate was sure, they both knew that someday he'd have to give up on her. The sooner the better, as far as she was concerned.

"My whole morning has been messed up!" she announced to Betty Jane an hour later as they headed for lunch at the cafeteria. "First chapel, then being late for chem class, and then not getting my homework done for English. I hope the afternoon is a little more relaxed."

"Well, lunch is going to be ruined," said Betty Jane in an undertone.

"Why?"

"Here come Jean and Andrea."

"They won't try to sit with us, will they?"

"Who knows?" Betty Jane shrugged. She and Kate headed for an empty table and laid down their trays.

Andrea towed Jean over to the table. "Betty Jane, have you got the notes for English class? I missed it because I had to go talk to Pastor Walters."

"They're in my notebook. I'll get them for you when I'm finished eating. Sit down and join us. How did it go?"

"How did what go?"

"Your meeting with Pastor Walters."

"Oh, that. He was really sweet to me—he's such a nice man. He helped me a lot."

"He has a son who's really good-looking," Jean added helpfully.

"How did you find that out?"

"He showed us a picture of his family."

"That's nice," Kate said.

"So what does his son look like?" Betty Jane wanted to know.

"Oh . . . well, he looks a lot like John Perry, actually."

Kate held her napkin to her mouth and made a choking noise. Betty Jane giggled.

"Maybe you've noticed that Kate is not a member of the John Perry fan club."

"Who is?" Jean quipped. "But he is cute. And anyway, we all know why Kate pretends to hate him so much."

"Why's that?" asked Andrea.

"Shut up, Jean," Kate warned. "It's not true."

Jean ignored her. "Last year, before you came here," she told Andrea, "John Perry was a senior here and Kate had the worst kind of crush on him."

"That's a lie!"

Betty Jane and Andrea were obviously enjoying the entertainment. "Go on," Andrea urged. "What happened?"

"Well, she chased him for months—all fall quarter, anyway—and finally one night there was this Christmas party, and Kate was just crazy to go with John, and —"

"I was never crazy to go anywhere with that *idiot*!"

Kate exclaimed. She slammed her milk glass on the table for emphasis and then had to set to work mopping up the spilled milk.

Jean was laughing so hard she could hardly continue the story. "Anyway, of course he didn't ask her, but they were both there and Kate was bugging John like crazy, stealing his shoes and dumping ice down his neck and kid stuff like that, and finally John told her in front of everybody to stop flirting with him and leave him alone, that she was just too childish for him."

Kate still held the wad of wet napkins in her hand. "Jean, I wish you'd just shut your mouth. Maybe you don't have anything better to do than go spreading lies about other people, but I've got better things to do than sit here and listen to your cheap gossip!" Jumping out of her seat, Kate kicked her chair over, flung the wet napkins at Jean's tray, and stormed out of the cafeteria. The milk-spattered Jean yelled one parting comment, and the boys at the next table started up a round of applause in response to Kate's performance.

The sounds of clapping and laughter were still burning Kate's ears long after she'd left the cafeteria behind. But it was Jean's final words that made her cheeks flame. "I just love your Christian attitude," she'd said.

What does she know about Christianity? Kate fumed. What right does she have to judge me? She's certainly not in any position to throw stones!

The truth, the real reason why Jean's comment hurt, thudded against her brain, but she refused to let it in.

Kate made her way at last to the washroom. For once it was empty. She stood in front of the mirror, her cheek pressed against the cool metal wall of the stall. The urge to cry, to scream, passed away and left her feeling drained and disappointed in herself.

I really thought I'd outgrown that, she reflected ruefully. Most of the time I can at least hold on to my temper.

Even that consolation, though, couldn't hide the fact that she often heard herself saying things that hit people as directly as a slap across the face. Kate liked to think of herself as being calm, cool, and controlled, but the truth, as she well knew, was that she was best known for her sharp tongue. What made it worse this time was that she had lost control and made a fool of herself—and that every word of Jean's story had been true.

She's right, Kate told herself reluctantly. Not just about John—that doesn't matter now—but about me being a Christian. If I am—if it's real—people should be able to see it in me. And they sure can't.

Two girls came into the washroom, laughing loudly. "What's the matter, Kate?" Sue Willis asked when they saw the older girl leaning against the wall.

"Oh, nothing much," Kate replied. Sue and Marcy went into the stalls, still talking loudly to each other. Kate took a long look into the mirror. She saw there a tall, slim girl, long, dark hair pulled back into that defiant ponytail, neat blue-checked shirt tucked into pleated blue skirt. A stranger.

She turned to go.

Her hurrying footsteps took her unseeing through crowds up to the second story. Earlier, she'd passed the counselor's office where Pastor Walters was meeting students, and there had been a lineup of students outside. Now there was nobody. Kate glanced at the clock. Twelve-twenty.

". . . your Christian attitude." What Christian attitude? Kate wondered wryly. Me, a Christian? That's a laugh.

Without thinking, she sat down on the chair nearest the office door. She tried not to hold on to her disturbing thoughts. She'd been discouraged like this before: experience told her that by the end of the afternoon she'd have forgotten.

Just then the office door swung open. Pastor Walters

was letting Bob MacNeil out. "I'll be praying for you, Bob," he said. Kate tried to smile back at Bob and hoped that he was too absorbed in his own troubles to wonder what she, the original goody-two-shoes, was doing there.

Pastor Walters looked from Bob to his watch to Kate. "I still have a few minutes left, young lady, although I have to be out of here by quarter to one. Would you like to step inside?"

I've let myself in for it now, Kate realized. I'll have to tell him about what I was thinking this morning—about Week of Prayer not doing any good.

She sat down and introduced herself. "It's not that I have any particular problem, sir. It's just that I was wondering, well, about Week of Prayer. Whether it does any good."

"I certainly hope it does," Pastor Walters said seriously. "What do you mean, Kate?"

"Well, a lot of the kids get really excited when there's a call. Even though they've been baptized and have done it all before, they give their hearts to the Lord—but it never seems to last. Nobody really sticks with it."

Pastor Walters leaned forward. "That's a common complaint. I think the problem is that many people do make a serious commitment to Christ, but they don't know how to keep that alive. They need to develop a real relationship with Christ, and this is done by—"

"Prayer, Bible study, and sharing your faith. I've heard that so many times." Kate glanced up uncertainly, afraid she had been rude. "Of course, I know it's true . . ."

To her surprise, Pastor Walters was laughing. "Perhaps that's the problem, Kate. You—and your friends—have heard these things so many times that they've lost their impact. I hope you won't forget that even if you've grown up with the gospel, there comes a time when one has to decide whether or not to take it seriously."

Kate swallowed. "I guess what I want is some kind of step-by-step how-to book."

"There are plenty of those around but the best one I know is found right in the Bible." He took a slip of paper from the desk and scribbled something on it. Handing it to Kate, he said, "You may find this more of a description than a prescription, but I hope it will be helpful."

"Thank you, sir," said Kate. She didn't have the faintest idea what he meant about descriptions and prescriptions, but she knew she'd sound stupid if she asked. She got up.

Pastor Walters held the door open for her. "I'll be praying for you, Kate," he said.

The last remark was overheard by Barry Armstrong, who was passing in the hall and paused to give Kate a searching glance. She blushed and looked away.

So I got caught going to see the pastor, she thought. The best she could hope was that the story wouldn't get around.

* * * * *

If You wanted to get my attention, Lord, You certainly picked an unusual way to do it. But I guess I needed it . . . anyway, I got into trouble for not listening to the teacher in class after that. I've been putting off thinking about You for a long time now, but I did enough thinking yesterday to make up for all the past seventeen years. In fact, I was so absentminded that when Mom came home she caught me with my ponytail still up!

Pastor Walters did make a call today. Only this one was for people who had already given their hearts to You but who wanted to commit themselves to a serious, day-by-day relationship with You. I wonder if I gave him the idea. Anyway, I stood up. Of course, so did almost everyone else, but I really meant it. I'm really going to try. Pastor Walters wrote "2 Peter 1:5-7" on a piece of paper and gave it to me. I read it, but it doesn't seem to make much sense. I hope it will become clearer.

The reason I'm writing to You is that I've always had trouble with serious praying—my mind wanders and I don't say the things I want to say. I was looking through my old shoebox of "treasures"—mostly letters and poems—and I realized that when I really want to think something through, I write it down. And if I have anything important to say to someone, I usually write a letter, even if the person is as close as the next desk.

So I'm trying this. I hope You understand. Please help me.

All my love,
Kate

BASKETBALL SEASON
Practice Makes Virtue

Dear God,   *November 12*

   The past few weeks have been quite an experience! Some things have been just too great to be believed. There's been a lot of changes. But one thing still worries me . . . it's me. I'm not sure I act any more like a Christian, although I feel a lot more like one. What's the answer, Lord? I can't make myself good. Can You do it?

   If I haven't learned the answer to that yet, I have, at least, learned a few other things this month.

* * * * *

Kate rolled off her stomach onto her back and gazed at the ceiling. Time for another school day to begin. This business of getting up early was still a little strange to her, but she managed to pull it off successfully at least four mornings a week. And morning devotions really were going well. The Bible had never seemed interesting to her before—but then, she'd never really tried to read it before. Now she had a ragged notebook full of her thoughts and discoveries—and those letters to God! Nobody else would understand about them, that was for sure. Betty Jane would think she deserved to be locked in a padded cell.

Kate glanced at the clock. Two minutes until the bus was due to leave. The bus driver had gotten so used to her chronic lateness that he habitually waited for a minute at the bus stop. Kate grabbed her jacket and her khaki knapsack and rushed out the door. She arrived at the foot of the street at the same time the bus did, and the driver grinned at her and shook his head.

"Right under the bar!" he said.

Kate smiled. "I always make it, don't I?" She dropped in her fare and sat down.

"School—the same old grind every day!" Betty Jane complained as Kate hung her coat up in the locker at school.

"Well, we have something to look forward to today, at least," Kate assured her.

"What's that?" Betty Jane asked skeptically.

"The sports event of the year! The great junior-senior basketball game!"

"Oh, that! Well, just because it's an unofficial scrub game in the parking lot with makeshift basketball nets doesn't mean it's not an important event. Of course, the game will be newsworthy just because of the seniors' most valuable player—the all-star Betty Jane Donovan!"

"You need a publicity agent," Kate decided. "You are definitely too modest."

Lunchtime found Kate in jeans and sneakers running frantically for the ball. At last Barry passed it to her, looking a little hopeless as he did so. She lobbed it desperately toward the net. It balanced on the rim, circled once, and fell—away from the net.

Terry Fields waved at her. "You're no star, kid, but you're definitely improving!"

"Pardon me, sir," Kate retorted, "but you should speak to a senior with more respect!" Terry dashed off into the fray, laughing. At least, Kate thought, he's friendly to the opposition.

Despite Kate's presence on the team, the seniors managed a narrow win. Grudging congratulations from the juniors filled the air as the seniors filed into biology class—late again. Only Nancy, whose definition of ladylike behavior didn't include playing lunchtime basketball, was sitting in the lab. She looked smug. Mr.

Hanson looked frustrated.

"If I'd known about the lure of basketball I would never have agreed to teach a class after lunch," he announced. "Well, I understand the attraction and I sympathize with your desire to prove senior superiority—*but* you cannot afford to lose classtime, and if this happens again you will suffer the consequences. Now, Betty Jane, what do you remember about DNA?"

Even the most unathletic of the students heard about the next day's game. The seniors, having proved themselves the better of the upperclassmen, had contrived to arrange a contest between themselves and the faculty. Two or three of the teachers still played soccer or baseball in neighborhood leagues, but the best of the seniors—Bob, Barry, and Jean—were confident of success.

The game was exciting. Kate spent a lot of her time on the sidelines, since Barry had kindly told her not to sabotage the team's chances by playing too enthusiastically. The seniors' case was hopeless anyway, though. The teachers had a good strong start and they gained momentum. They won, 36 to 12.

The seniors didn't stay around to congratulate their opponents. Nor did the girls pause to change back into their skirts as they usually did. Instead, the whole class moved in one united rush to the lab. Kate, the last in, closed the door and locked it behind her. "We made it!" she exclaimed.

The bell rang, and the seniors sat primly in their seats. Five minutes ticked by to the sound of muffled giggles. At last the door handle rattled, the key scraped in the lock, and Mr. Hanson strode confidently in and opened his book onto the desk before him. But before one word could be said about DNA, Barry rose and addressed the teacher.

"Sir, you cannot afford to lose classtime. If this happens again . . . "

The whole class chimed in on the final phase, "YOU

WILL SUFFER THE CONSEQUENCES!"

Mr. Hanson smilingly conceded the point, and the seniors felt that they had at least won some ground back.

They stood in the parking lot after school, discussing the game. "Well, gang," Kate said, interrupting a technical argument between Jeff and Bob, "the one thing you can say is that we played well and we did the best we could. So let's celebrate!"

Jean turned to her. "What do you know about it? You didn't even play half the game! Just sat on the sidelines and got in the way."

Kate forced a smile. "Well, that was probably the best thing for the team."

"You can say that again," Jean shot back. "In fact, if you hadn't played at all, we probably would have won!"

No, God, please. Keep hold of me. If I don't say anything, I'll be sulking. If I say something, it'll be the wrong thing. "Well, at least I'm improving—I think!"

Barry came to her rescue. "That's true—today she hit the backboard!"

Kate slapped him playfully on the arm with her notebook, and Jean, by some miracle, subsided.

Jeff and Barry accompanied Kate to the bus stop. "Don't mind Jean," Barry said kindly. "Her mouth should be permanently closed."

"Wired shut," Jeff agreed grimly.

"Oh, she's not that bad," Kate said. She didn't feel particularly angry anymore. "She's got a right to talk—she's good."

"No better than Betty Jane," Barry decided. "Jean would be better if she were taller."

"Everyone tells me I should be good at basketball," Kate said wistfully. She didn't like revealing her own shortcomings, but in this case they were pretty obvious anyway. She was afraid of what she might say if they kept talking about Jean. "I'm as tall as some of the guys, but I just haven't got the coordination. I'm awkward with the ball."

"Well," Barry said thoughtfully, "you could practice shooting by yourself now and then. But the best thing you can do is to keep playing as much as you can. Practice makes perfect."

"After all," Jeff added, "you've got to look at it—our games aren't organized sports or anything, so there's always room for everyone to improve. Nobody's perfect yet."

"Thanks, I'll try to remember that. And you remember it next time you lose a game because of me!"

They climbed on the bus, and Kate sat at the back with the boys. Before this, she'd always seemed to have little to say to them, but lately she was getting to know them much better.

"It's the Senior Syndrome," Betty Jane explained later. "We're united, we've got class spirit, and we know we'll all be leaving each other soon, so we get closer to each other."

"That's true," Kate agreed. "I even find Jean more human. It was always so easy just to label her and Bob as 'the bad kids' and forget it."

"One other reason could be that our class is so much smaller now. So many people left last year to go to public school or boarding academy! Eight people is a pretty small graduating class. Mr. Ames says it's the smallest the academy has ever had . . . or is it just in the past twenty years? I'm not sure. But anyway . . . "

Kate's mind was far away from the size of their graduating class. "It's not just Jean," she broke in.

"What's that?"

"Well, you know . . . misjudging people. I never got to know Barry before, because he always seemed so sure of himself, so perfect. And Jeff was just—"

"His sidekick. I know," Betty Jane said, suddenly serious. "His family is over at my place an awful lot, because our parents are such good friends. Jeff likes hanging around with Barry, but sometimes he's scared that nobody ever sees *him*. He's shy, in a way."

"I didn't know that," Kate said.

"Anyway, it was nice of Barry to kind of stick up for you today," Betty Jane continued. "If I'd been you, I would have creamed Jean."

"Well, I didn't have any more napkins around to throw at her! And I'm tired of making scenes."

"She deserves it. She's going to get in big trouble someday. . . . Have you heard anything more about her and Bob?"

Kate was silent. She *had* overheard some talk—but why let it go any further? "Nobody's told me anything. Anyway, it's kind of a sick subject," she added hastily, trying not to think about how much she'd like to pass the story along. "There are more exciting things to talk about."

"That's true," Betty agreed. "Like graduation. Only seven months to go!"

* * * * *

I've been trying to put the things I've learned about You into practice, but I'm not always successful. Sometimes I get so angry! And I don't usually catch myself in time. The few times I do, it seems to be Your doing instead of mine.

I guess that all I can do is to keep spending time with You and getting to know You better. I want to learn to "pray without ceasing." Is that possible? I'm sure I can't gossip or be angry with people if I'm thinking about You.

Thank You for everything You've done for me so far!

All my love,
Kate

RINGING OUT THE OLD
Live and Learn

Dear God,   *December 31*

I've got quite a pile of letters to You stacked up from the last months of this year. And, somehow, I feel that You've been answering. The thing I've found most striking, lately, is how I've been understanding more and more things that have been only theory before. I've learned so much from my Bible study, yet at times I feel like I've learned even more from my attempts to do Your will.

Anyway, it certainly has been an interesting year!

* * * * *

Kate ran down the church stairs to the youth auditorium. Hanging up her coat, she almost bumped into Jean, who was changing from her boots to her shoes.

"Oh—'scuse me," Kate said. "Hi, Jean, how are you doing?"

"All right," Jean said darkly. "Considering the way things are going."

"What do you mean?"

"You should know by now. If you don't, I'm sure someone will be glad to fill you in." Jean finished buckling her shoes and walked past Kate into the auditorium. Catching Kate's questioning glance, she turned and said, "Forget it, OK?"

Shrugging, Kate followed Jean into the youth room. What can I do? Kate wondered. I've tried "loving" her, but what does that really mean? I'm sure she doesn't want any condescending pity. Anyway, whatever I'm doing seems to be wrong.

She sat down next to Betty Jane and Marcy.

Curiosity overcame her. "Betty Jane?"

"H'mm?"

"What's Jean so upset about?"

Betty Jane smiled wryly. "Where have you been lately? The all-time big news at school Thursday was Jean's visit to the principal's office."

"What for?"

"She and Bob got caught in the darkroom."

"Oh?" prompted Kate, trying not to ask what they'd been doing.

"Use your imagination," Marcy volunteered helpfully. "Bob hasn't been seen at school since it happened, but Jean sure got told off."

"Oh, well. That's too bad." Kate decided it was about time for a change of subject, but just then the song service started.

The program went by quickly, and soon it was time for the lesson study. That week's lesson was about love—loving one another. Kate listened eagerly, trying to find the answers to her questions.

Mr. Phillips made it clear that Christian love, "agape" love, was a principle, a way of acting, rather than a feeling. Then he tossed out a question. "How do we love? If we know that we must love everybody, and we choose to do so, how do we express that love?"

Barry's hand shot up. "By doing what's best for other people."

Kate, sitting next to Nancy and writing notes on the back of her quarterly, looked at Jean. She remembered school yesterday, when she had met Jean in the hall as she came into school. Kate had made some joke about the freshmen, who had lavishly covered the school halls with Christmas decorations. "They'll learn to be senior scrooges before long," Jean replied, laughing, and added, "Ready for the English test?"

Such a silly little conversation, Kate mused, the same kind I might have had with Betty Jane. But Jean responded just the way Betty Jane would have. It's the closest I've ever felt to her.

Terry, Barry, and Laurie were still discussing love. Kate's hand shot up.

"Yes, Kate?" Mr. Phillips said.

"Well . . . I just thought . . . it isn't really enough to love people, is it? I mean, none of us is really sure what love is. What people really want is to be liked, don't they? So maybe we should 'like one another.'"

Barry disagreed. "That's impossible, Kate. You can't like everybody. Some people you're naturally attracted to, and some you aren't. We can't be responsible for that. We have to love people whether or not we like them."

"That's not quite what I mean," Kate replied. "I mean we have to learn to treat people as though we like them."

"But liking is a natural response," argued Barry. "You can't force yourself to feel it."

Terry jumped in. "I think I see what you're both saying. Barry's right. We don't naturally like everybody. But what Kate means is that we should act toward everybody as we would if we liked them, right?"

"Yes!" laughed Kate in relief.

"Then what you call 'liking' is just one very important part of what we've been calling love," Barry summed up.

After Sabbath school Mr..Phillips pulled Kate aside. He beckoned to Betty Jane and Barry to come over too.

"Christmas is just around the corner," he told them. "I have an idea for a special Sabbath school program that we can plan for the last Sabbath before Christmas holidays. I think it would be a good time to have a Visitors' Day program, and I'd like you kids to be in charge of it."

"Us?" gulped Betty Jane, but Barry was more practical. "What exactly do you have in mind, sir?" he asked.

"I'll leave that up to you," Mr. Phillips said. "Check back with me later this week and let me know what you've planned." He strode away.

Kate was immediately inspired, and her flow of ideas came so enthusiastically that Barry finally had to stem the tide by saying, "Look, let's plan a meeting for Monday after school and get our ideas down on paper, OK?"

"Right, chief," Kate responded.

"Ever consider going into politics, Barry?" asked Betty with a grin.

Barry winked. "Would you vote for me?"

The next week was, predictably, a busy one. After school on Monday, Betty Jane and Kate met with Barry. Their meeting lasted so long that the teachers ordered them out of the building and they had to continue the meeting at Betty Jane's house. Their main problem was that Kate and Betty Jane found something funny about almost everything that was discussed, and their combined force managed to draw even the businesslike Barry into fits of giggling. Betty Jane invited them to stay for supper, and they continued to make their plans. It was long past dark when Barry and Kate caught the bus, and Kate arrived home feeling tired and happy from the day's activities.

Tuesday was not as pleasant. Bob MacNeil returned to school, and the tension between him and Jean was thick enough to cut with a knife. In the middle of the second period—Mr. Hanson's chemistry class—the principal's secretary knocked on the door. She had a brief consultation with Mr. Hanson, who hated to have his classes interrupted, and then Mr. Hanson turned around and announced, "Bob, you're wanted in the principal's office."

Bob lifted himself out of his seat gracelessly and swaggered to the door. A muffled snicker came from somewhere in the classroom, but the students exchanged worried glances.

Chemistry class faded into English class, and Bob did not return. In the middle of English, again there came a knock on the door, and again it was Freida. This time Jean was called to leave. Pausing only to grab her purse, she left the room without looking at anyone. The atmosphere was tense after she had gone.

By unspoken agreement, the six remaining seniors sat together at lunchtime, and there was only one topic of conversation.

"I think they'll both be expelled," Jeff opined.

Betty Jane thought perhaps they would only be suspended. Andrea, who was new at the academy, didn't see why anything should happen to them.

"Well, the reason I think they'll be kicked out," Jeff explained, "is that they've both been in trouble before. Bob's been suspended twice before, and I think Jean has once."

"Speak of the devil," Barry said quietly. Jean was entering the cafeteria, sitting down at a nearby vacant table with her back to the others. There was a moment of strained silence.

"We can make room for her, can't we?" Kate asked weakly. She saw Barry and Jeff exchange doubtful glances, and she turned to Andrea for support.

"Jean!" Andrea called. "Come over here!"

"Scoot over, and turn your trays sideways," said Betty Jane. Jean, who had been hesitating, saw them make room for her and came over. She said nothing as she laid her tray down.

"Where's Bob?" Nancy asked after a pause.

Jean looked down at her tray. "I don't know, and I couldn't care less. He just left, anyway. Please go ahead with what you were talking about. If it was about me, I just won't listen."

Nobody could think of anything to say.

Kate went to bed uneasy on Tuesday night. Worries about Bob and Jean tumbled around with plans for the Sabbath school program in her brain. It was late when she fell asleep and early when she awoke. Rather than reaching for her Bible when she awoke, as she had been trying to get into the habit of doing, she rolled over in bed and went back to sleep.

When she awoke again, it was too late to take time for devotions. She prayed silently and hurriedly as she made her bed, then joined her parents for breakfast. For once she wasn't late for the bus, and an empty seat next to Barry guaranteed that she didn't have to sit alone.

A feeling of impending doom hung over the school all day, but the storm refused to break. Bob was nowhere to be found, and Jean left after lunch. Two of the seniors hung around the principal's office talking to Freida all through their free period, but returned with no news to tell the class.

Barry, Betty Jane, and Kate met after school to discuss the Sabbath school again. "I was hoping we could get some of the kids who don't usually come to church to come for this program—like Bob. But that doesn't seem too likely now," Barry said.

"There are still lots of others," Kate pointed out. "Andrea told me today that she might come. And there are some in the other classes who don't usually go."

"Besides," Betty Jane added, "all the kids have non-Adventist friends in their neighborhoods."

"Yes," Barry agreed. "But will they bring them?"

Kate was home in time for supper this time. "Where have you been?" her mother asked.

"At school, planning for our Sabbath school program. What about you? Just get home?"

"Of course," Mrs. Nichol said with a sigh. "Whatever you decide to do in life, Kate, don't be an elementary school teacher at Christmas."

"I thought that was supposed to be the time you got all the hugs and kisses and heartwarming rewards."

"It's the time you get to plan the Christmas program, and I defy anyone to tell me that there's anything heartwarming about that!"

Kate laughed and began to set the table for supper.

Homework and phone calls took up the rest of Kate's evening. As she lay in bed, she was grateful for a day that had had fewer problems and worries in it than the day before.

I really can't think of one single thing that went wrong, she mused. I didn't lose my temper with anyone, I don't think I said anything I shouldn't have said, and for once I got all my work done. I guess I could call this a successful day.

But something still troubled her. There was a feeling of emptiness, of incompleteness, about her almost-perfect day. Finally she pinpointed it.

I didn't have devotions this morning or this evening, she realized. And I wasn't thinking about God today— hardly at all. Yet I still had a good day. Does that mean I don't really need Him?

The thought troubled her. Surely she was dependent on God for any success she had. But if she found she could "be good" without Him, what was wrong?

Well, for one thing, she thought, my being good probably wouldn't last more than a couple days without Him. But there's something else, too. What's the purpose of my being a Christian? Surely it's not just an elaborate system to keep me from losing my temper or criticizing people. The purpose of my Christianity is to bring me into a relationship with Jesus. If I haven't been close to Him, no matter how "good" my day has been, it's been a failure.

Kate was struck by the new idea. Of course! It wasn't enough just to overcome bad habits—they had to be replaced by a joyful, growing relationship with Jesus. If that wasn't there, nothing was.

Kate turned on the light and reached for her Bible. After searching through the Bible for a long time, she finally found the story she was looking for.

"When the unclean spirit is gone out of a man, he walketh through dry places, seeking rest, and findeth none. Then he saith, I will return into my house from whence I came out; and when he is come, he findeth it empty, swept, and garnished. Then goeth he, and taketh with himself seven other spirits more wicked than himself, and they enter in and dwell there: and the last state of that man is worse than the first."

Kate put her bookmark in the place—Matthew 12:43-45—and pulled out her notebook and pen. I must remember, she thought, that it's not enough to get rid of some of my old problems. I have to replace them with something positive.

She scribbled a few lines in the notebook, and then turned out the light.

The days slipped by. Bob and Jean were both suspended until after Christmas. Plans for the Christmas Visitors' Day grew more frantic as the day drew nearer. Kate had suggested that two or three people should give a short personal testimony, and Betty Jane and Barry had immediately suggested that since it had been Kate's idea, Kate ought to be one of the volunteers. On the Thursday night before the program, Kate was sitting at her desk, trying to decide how all the things that had happened to her since fall Week of Prayer could best be put down on paper. The phone rang in the middle of her thoughts, and she ran to get it.

"Hi, Kate. Listen, I was just wondering—"

"Betty Jane! This is the fourth time you've called me tonight!"

"Well, excuse me! We have only got two days left, you know. And I found out that Sue can't do special music because she's got to be out of town. So what will we do?"

"We've already got Mrs. Williams doing one, haven't we?"

"Yes, but I wanted to have two. We need a lot of music in the program."

"Well . . . " Kate reviewed hurriedly all the musically talented people she knew. "Try Terry Fields. I've never heard him sing in public before, but I know he can.

You'll probably have to talk him into it."

"Kate! I hardly know him!"

"OK, don't worry about it. I'll call him, and then I'll call you back and let you know what he says."

"Thanks, Kate. You're an angel, you know that? A real lifesaver."

"We're all in this thing together, kid."

Smiling, Kate resigned herself to an evening of interruptions and began dialing Terry's number.

* * * * *

Standing up in front of all those people I've known for years and giving my testimony was a real learning experience. Somehow I had to find the right way to say all the things I'd been learning, and even if I didn't do anyone else any good, it did me a lot of good to organize my thoughts that way.

So many of the things I've learned—about love, about needing to be close to You every day—are things that I think I've read in Sabbath school quarterlies all my life. But I don't think they meant a thing to me until I'd experienced them. I didn't realize that trying to do Your will was going to be so revealing, but I'm certainly glad it has been. It's good to know that when a person tries to follow You, the process of following teaches us just about everything we need to know.

I'm not going to make any New Year's resolutions, Lord, because thanks to You I don't need them. I'll only make the resolution that I made every day—to live this day (and this year) in Your joyous presence!

All my love,
Kate

TIME FLIES
This Is Temperance?

Dear God,   *January 29*
Another year is well under way, and midterm exams are just behind me. I can't wait to see what You have planned for me in the year ahead. The first few weeks of it have certainly been busy—as usual! And I thank You for being with me throughout them. If I hadn't learned a few valuable lessons, I would have gotten so carried away in my many activities that I might have lost sight of You. In fact, for a little while I almost did.

* * * * *

Kate came into the classroom on the first school day of the new year to find the air buzzing. Everybody seemed to be talking at once (Mr. Ames hadn't yet entered), and Kate couldn't figure out what was going on. "All right, all right," she shouted above the din, "I know you're all glad to see me, but you don't have to make *that* much fuss about it!" Her words were drowned in a chorus of catcalls, and she sat down laughing.

"Seriously, though," she said to Betty Jane, "what's the latest disaster?" A quick glance around the classroom told her that Bob and Jean had returned—not, it seemed, on the friendliest terms with each other—and she wondered what new catastrophe could have struck so early in the new term.

"I was just telling everybody," Betty Jane began in a tone of voice that hinted she'd been running into some opposition, "that our graduation is only six months away—less than six months, more like five months—and we haven't got a thing planned yet!"

"What do we have to plan?" Kate asked. "Doesn't the school take care of most of that stuff?"

"Sure, if all you want to do is march up the aisle and get a diploma," Betty Jane said.

"Well, what more do we need?" Jeff asked.

"I've just spent the last five minutes telling you!"

"I know," Jeff said. "But what I don't see is why all that stuff is necessary."

"All what stuff?" Kate interrupted. "Don't forget, I missed most of this."

"The problem is," Betty Jane began, "that we girls all want to have a party or a dinner or something afterward, and the guys don't want to support the idea."

"Not all the girls," Jean corrected. "I think it's a dumb idea. Why not just get our diplomas and get out of here?"

"Then that's four against three," Barry announced triumphantly, "and we win. No party."

"Wait a second," said Kate. "I have a vote too, don't forget. And I think it would be fun to have a party. That makes it four to four."

"I never noticed you guys hated parties so much before," Betty Jane said smoothly.

"It's not that we hate parties," Barry explained. "It's just that we hate to plan them, pay for them, and clean up after them."

"Look at what we're going to need," Jeff added. "Probably something big enough for all the teachers to come to, and our parents, and our dates." He scribbled quickly on a piece of paper. "That's thirty-nine people right there."

"All the teachers are married," Barry reminded him.

"That's right. Make that forty-six. What are we going to do for forty-six people? We'll need a place to have it in, food, entertainment, and loads of money."

"Why not just go out for pizza?" Kate asked.

"No way. If we're going to do this, we'll do it right," Betty Jane announced.

"Then let's not do it at all," Bob suggested.

The battle raged on all day, but by the time school was out, Betty Jane had won Barry, Jeff, and Jean over to the cause, and Bob said he didn't want to vote against everyone else.

"So it's unanimous!" Betty Jane declared, and everybody laughed.

"You mean it's unanimous because four people voted Yes and four people were forced to vote Yes?" Barry asked.

"That still makes eight," Betty Jane said with a smug smile.

The rest of the week was taken up with the election of class officers. Betty Jane modestly declined the job of president and said she preferred the humble role of secretary-treasurer.

"So that she has all the real power," complained Barry, who had been elected president.

Everybody refused to be nominated for sergeant-at-arms, so Mr. Ames—who had stepped into the act to prevent utter chaos—drew a name from a box, having previously stated that if the person whose name was drawn did not accept the office he or she would also not accept the honor of marching with the class and receiving a diploma.

"Mr. Ames proves once again that force gets results," Jeff whispered to Kate as Nancy reluctantly accepted the job.

The position of valedictorian was left vacant until after final exams, but when Betty Jane nominated Kate for class pastor, Barry said, "Better not. She's most likely going to be valedictorian anyway."

"Don't say that!" Kate demanded, embarrassed.

"I'm just going by the existing records," Barry insisted. Jeff was voted in as class pastor.

Betty Jane announced that her first official duty would be to form a fund-raising committee of eight members, which would hold its first meeting during algebra class the next day. Because of some opposition from Mr. Ames, the faculty sponsor and math teacher, the time of the meeting had to be changed, but, as Betty pointed out, a class period was the only time you could be sure of getting everyone there. It was decided that since the elections had taken place in algebra class, trigonometry would be sacrificed instead.

So Kate, along with all the others, got pulled into the whirl of activities leading up to the crowning event of the school year—graduation.

In church the following week, Mrs. Fields, the personal ministries leader, drew Kate aside.

"We've been planning to open up a temperance booth in the shopping mall," she explained, "with displays and literature and a film that we're going to show. They have a little room that you can use for free, you know, for films and things, and we thought we might be able to get a little television set to show videos on—that would attract people to the display. We need some high school students to sit at the booth—I was wondering if you'd like to help."

"Well, I have midterms coming up, and I'm helping plan some fund-raising for the grad . . ." Mrs. Fields looked disappointed. Any student she asked would have midterms coming up, Kate realized. And there wasn't really that much fund-raising activity coming up in the next few weeks. "I think I can make time for it, though," Kate said. "When are you planning to do it?"

Kate found herself doing her first turn of duty at the booth on a Sunday night. She was beginning to be worried. Midterms were one week away, and, as usual, she had procrastinated. Untidy piles of notes from the first four months of the year waited on the desk at home, but she hadn't yet done any studying. She sat at the booth with Terry and Sue. (At least they aren't seniors, she thought enviously; they've got it easy.) And she talked with people who stopped to look at the display, and handed out literature and invited passersby to see the film and debated with two teenage boys about smoking. And she worried. When she got home, though, it was too late to study. There was still the next day's homework to do.

"And I've got to do this Tuesday and Thursday nights as well!" she told her mother in despair.

"You should have given it more thought when Mrs. Fields asked you to do it. And you should have either told her you couldn't do it, or realized how busy you'd be and studied earlier." Mrs. Nichol smiled at her daughter. "It's kind of late for that kind of advice, isn't it? Just do your best and try to learn something from it."

Monday night Kate actually managed to study a little. She was interrupted only four times, twice by Terry calling to make arrangements for the temperance display the next night, and twice by Betty Jane calling to make plans for a bake sale on Thursday. Tuesday night Kate decided the most sensible thing she could do was to bring her books to the mall with her. She tried to study as she sat behind the table, but she was continually being interrupted by people coming over to talk. At last Terry said gently, "People are less likely to come look at the display if they get the feeling they're disturbing us. Maybe we should try to give them our full attention while we're here."

"That's fine for you to say," snapped Kate. "I'm a senior and I have midterm exams next week and this is my only study time!"

"Hold on a second. I'm a junior and I have exams next week too. Don't forget that it's my mother who's running this show and I have to be here every single night."

"I'm sorry," Kate said, her voice trembling a little. "It's just that I haven't done any studying at all yet, and I don't know when I'm going to do it."

"I understand," Terry said. "What I don't understand is why you didn't study last week."

"I'm just a hopeless procrastinator. But I'll get it done sometime. Sorry I got mad."

What's wrong with me? she wondered. I thought I'd gotten over this business of flying off the handle. And what a person to do it to—Terry, who's always so nice to me. I've never seen him get mad at anybody.

"God, this week is turning out to be a real mess." That was the only prayer that Kate had time for on Wednesday. Betty Jane was tearing around school, crusading for donations to the bake sale and for people to come and help sell. All the seniors were pressed into service, and when Kate tried to back out, it was Betty Jane who lost her cool.

"You really haven't been a lot of help, have you? We need you, and you'd better be there!"

"I can't promise anything. You don't have any idea what kind of pressure I'm under."

Betty Jane almost dropped her books. "You're under no more pressure than the rest of us, except that you think you have to maintain your precious 4.0 GPA! Let me just tell you, you're no better than anyone else, and you'll have to pitch in and work just as hard as all the rest of us!"

Kate was suddenly exhausted. Quarreling with her best friend? Things had really gotten out of hand. "I'm sorry B.J. It's just that I'm a little behind in my work. I see what you mean, and I'll try to help."

"Good girl. Oh, by the way, can you drive me around tonight to pick up the things people are baking for us? Some people said they couldn't drop them off at the school, and I promised I'd pick them up."

It was fortunate for both girls that Betty Jane had to run off just then to talk to somebody. If she had heard Kate's response to her request, a new and more exciting quarrel would have been under way.

Why did I ever get a driver's license? Kate wondered

as she sat in the car outside the Williams' house. And why does Betty Jane make promises that she can keep only by having me drive her around?

Betty Jane had promised to be "just a second" at each house, so Kate didn't bother to come in. Hoping that the stops really would turn out to be quick ones, she hadn't brought anything to study in the car. The seconds ticked by, turning too soon into minutes. At last Betty Jane emerged.

"Only two more stops!" Betty Jane announced cheerfully.

"Where?"

"One to the Armstrongs'. . ."

"Wait a second. Why can't Barry bring it to school?"

"Because it's a very big cake and Barry rides the bus."

"Well, we'll get that last. Barry's only a few blocks from me. Where's the other place?"

"The Kenneys'."

Kate applied the brakes abruptly. "They don't even live in town!" she exclaimed.

"Oh, it's only a little way," Betty Jane coaxed. "Besides, they don't have a car, so there's no other way of getting it. And you know how good Mrs. Kenney's brownies are."

"We're selling them, not eating them," Kate grumbled, but she turned left and headed out the highway.

At the Kenneys', Betty Jane insisted that Kate come in. Kate was about to protest that it was getting late, when a glance at her watch told her that it was already too late to do any studying that evening. "And Mrs. Kenney would be so hurt if you didn't come in for a glass of milk and a brownie," Betty Jane said. "She loves young people, and she doesn't get out very often, living way out here, so she just loves it when people come to visit."

The Kenneys' warm kitchen was the only place where Kate had felt relaxed all week. She was telling Mr. Kenney about the temperance booth and how hard she was working on it.

"Temperance, eh? I used to be president of the Temperance Club for a long time when I was a young fellow. Didn't realize how important it was until I found out that there's a whole lot more to temperance than just not drinkin' and not smokin'."

"Yes, sir," Kate replied automatically. Mrs. Fields had given them a lecture on that very topic before they began their work.

"Poor child!" Mrs. Kenney said suddenly. "You're almost falling asleep!"

Kate looked up quickly, then laughed at herself. "I guess we'd better be moving on," she said. "It's pretty late. We're probably keeping you folks up, too."

"I hope you can get back to town with no trouble," said Mrs. Kenney, pulling aside the curtain to look out the window. "It's working up quite a storm out there."

Sure enough, snow was blowing all over the road when Kate and Betty Jane, loaded down with boxes of brownies, pulled away from the cozy little house. Kate's car crawled along, the driver leaning forward and peering through the windshield in hopes of seeing a patch of road.

The situation was no better on the city streets, and Kate was trembling a little when she pulled up in front of her own house.

"I'll have to get my dad to drive you home," she said to Betty Jane, "or you can stay here for the night. I don't want to drive in this, and I'm sure my folks don't want either their only car or their only daughter out in the storm."

Betty Jane agreed, and decided to stay with Kate for the night. "I'll call Barry and tell him that if he can't bring that cake on the bus tomorrow, he'll just have to walk to school with it."

"That raises another interesting question," Kate's mother said. "How do you girls plan to get all the baked goods you've collected to school tomorrow?"

"Oh, dear." Betty Jane's resources weren't equal to this final difficulty. "Maybe my mom could come up here and pick us up."

"No, that's too much trouble," Mrs. Nichol decided. "If you don't mind getting to school very early, you can come with Harry and me."

"Maybe," Kate said hopefully, "the storm will have gotten so bad by morning that school will be canceled."

Normally, Kate loved to have Betty Jane spend the night. But under the present circumstances, a night of gossiping until 3:00 A.M. lost its appeal. Once the lights were out and the house was silent, though, Kate abandoned all hope of sleep.

"So long as I've got you here," she said, interrupting Betty Jane's chatter about the bake sale, "do you mind if I tell you what's been bothering me?"

"I knew you would sooner or later."

"I guess it's been pretty obvious, hasn't it?"

"Well . . . what is it?"

Kate sighed and rehearsed the whole story of her responsibilities. "I *know* I shouldn't have put off studying for so long. But here I am in the middle of it now, and I hardly have time to breathe. I just feel like I'm falling apart because I never have time—"

"Time for what?"

"Time for anything," Kate finished. She really wanted to say, "I never have time for God." But something still made it difficult for her to talk to happy-go-lucky Betty Jane about her new experiences.

"Temperance," Betty Jane said irrelevantly.

"What?" Kate was annoyed. It seemed that every time she tried to talk to Betty Jane about anything serious, Betty Jane changed the subject.

"Like what Mr. Kenney said. There's more to temperance than what you eat and drink."

"I *know* that!"

"Don't bite my head off. I read this in a magazine. Temperance includes things like handling your time properly."

"Explain that."

"Well, sure, there are always going to be times when you're extra busy. But you have to plan your life ahead of time so you won't go under when that happens. You know, get your priorities straight and all. I can't remember it all, but you have to take control of your life, and that's self-control, and that's just a more modern word for temperance. Anyway, it's too late for you to organize your time now, I guess, but you could always keep it in mind for the next time. Oh, and about tomorrow. You don't have to work at the bake sale."

"Thanks, Betty Jane. I'll try to stop by for a little while anyway."

"Well, you did enough tonight, driving me around."

Miraculously, Betty Jane went to sleep then. But Kate lay awake. Temperance. Taking control of her life. Betty Jane was wrong. It wasn't too late to salvage even this week. Oh, it was too late to study for midterms, but it wasn't too late to get her priorities straight and make room for the really important things. She fumbled for her alarm clock and, despite her growing sleepiness, reset it to wake her half an hour earlier than she'd planned. Betty Jane could sleep through anything, and if she did happen to wake up, she'd just have to join in Kate's morning worship.

* * * * *

Well, I came through that one alive, Lord. And besides learning—again—that I need to spend time with You, I think I learned a general principle. Part of the Christian life is for me to control life instead of letting it control me. I don't mean that I should control it myself, Lord—only You can do that. What I mean is to take the responsibility into my own hands and turn things over to You as fast as they happen instead of letting the rush of events carry me away. When I get angry, I'll turn my anger over to You instead of letting myself blow up. When I get too busy, I'll turn my time over to You instead of letting myself get worn out and irritable. Thank You so much, Lord! I really needed that.

So now I have even more experience, and a broader definition of temperance. I wonder if I can persuade Mrs. Fields to use it in her next display?

All my love,
Kate

MIDWINTER BLUES
Peace and Patience

Dear God,   *February 28*
Thank You so much! Can You believe that at the end of this week—of this month—I'm thanking You? I can't! I could so easily have become discouraged, like I did before midterms. Only in this case my problem wasn't having too much to do. Maybe it was that I had too little. Anyway, I feel like I've come through the most important experience of my Christian life so far.

* * * * *

It was raining.

Not, Kate thought, that there was anything very newsworthy about that. It had been raining for so many days straight now that she had lost track of how long it had been since she had seen the sun.

"I think the weatherman should just stop giving out the forecast," she told her father. "Every evening on the news when it comes time for the forecast, they should just print a little blurb on the screen: More of the Same."

School had fallen into a midwinter grind. Even Betty Jane's unflagging enthusiasm for fund-raising had taken a downturn with the weather. After an endless procession of bake sales, craft sales, and cold-plate sales, the class had voted unanimously to suspend further activities until car-wash season rolled around. Teachers took advantage of the lull to assign extra homework and remind the senior class about the importance of final exams. "If you fail to prepare," Mr.

Ames told them, "you are preparing to fail." He repeated this gem of advice so many times that Barry suggested it should be adopted as their class motto. There was no doubt about the class aim: By this time it was simply "To Get Out of Here Alive."

Kate found that things were turning gray inside as well as outside. When she wrote her letters to God, she no longer had the feeling that anyone was reading them. Her prayers began to sound dull and repetitious. One morning during devotions she found herself thinking, to her own amazement, I guess I must have read most of the good stuff in the Bible by now—there doesn't seem to be anything else in there.

What could be wrong? She tried to search for the answer in prayer, but praying had become such a stale and flat activity that she began instead to make up excuses to avoid praying. "I need my sleep" was the best one she'd come up with so far.

One day things came to a head. Kate was sitting in Betty Jane's bedroom, watching Betty make up another of her endless lists—Things Needed for the Grad, this one was headed. Everything in Kate rebelled against being put down in the second column as Person to Find Entertainment. "Right now," she said aloud, "I'm hardly up to finding plastic forks and spoons."

"You couldn't do that anyway," Betty Jane said, chewing the top of her pen and concentrating on her list. "After Jeff got us all those paper plates for the cold-plate sale, I put him on to that job permanently. He's better than anyone else at getting stores to give donations—that curly brown hair and shy smile will do it every time."

"Sorry I haven't got the curls," Kate replied.

Betty Jane glanced up. "Lately you haven't got the smile, either. Is anything wrong?"

"I don't know," Kate responded. "I guess it's just the weather and everything getting me down."

"If you ask me, you're getting a little moody," Betty

Jane decided, and went back to her list.

She's right, Kate thought. I am moody. What a terrible way for a Christian to be. Up and down, up and down. Always up and down. First it was great, and I always felt good, but lately things have been on a real downturn. How can I get that old excitement back?

"Betty Jane, lend me a piece of paper, will you?"

"Great! Going to help me?" Betty Jane tore a sheet out of her exercise book. Kate made sure she had it firmly in her grasp before she replied.

"No, I'm not. I'm writing something for myself," she answered.

"Rats!" Betty Jane said.

Kate knew what she wanted to write. The words wove themselves in and out of the haunting melody turning round inside her head.

Father, Father, lead me, I don't ask to know the
*   way;*
Father, teach me all Your truth, I have no words to
*   say.*
No more words to say, Lord; No, no more words to
*   say.*
Nothing left for me, Lord; I only want Your way.

Father, Father, take me, I cannot see the road.
Father, Father, help me, I cannot bear the load.
Father, never leave me, I must keep holding on,
Only because I love You, for all my strength is gone.

Father, all my failures are heaped before my eyes;
Father, I'm so careless, so thoughtless, so unwise.
Let me take Your strength, Lord; my choice is firmly
*   made.*
There is no turning back now, though I may walk in
*   shade.*

The valley of the shadows of dull skies and long
*   days—*
I cry, "O lift me up, Lord, to fairer, brighter ways!"

But if this is Your path, Lord, I'll walk it, walk it true,
In light, in love, in You, Lord, there's nothing else to do.

"Going to show me?" Betty Jane asked when she saw Kate gazing at the paper.

"Maybe later," Kate said. She folded the poem and put it in her purse. "Now, can I have another piece of paper?"

"Oh, no. What is it this time?"

Kate smiled. "Just thought you might like someone to help you make lists."

That night, in her bedroom, Kate pulled out the poem and read it over again. That was exactly what she felt, she decided. Life could be pretty hard at times, but she had made a decision once and she was going to stick by it, come rain or shine.

She pulled her Bible toward her. "Sticking by it" meant that she would go on trying to study the Bible and trying to pray even when she didn't feel like it. She turned to the Gospel of John, her favorite book. Chapter 14. She'd memorized the whole chapter once in junior high, and it was all marked over with underlinings and highlights. She read through it, her mind sliding over most of the words, stopping to linger over a few cherished verses.

"Peace I leave with you, my peace I give unto you: not as the world giveth, give I unto you. Let not your heart be troubled, neither let it be afraid." She loved verse 27, the promise of peace. What did it mean, though—"not as the world giveth"? God's peace was supposed to be different from the peace of the world—but how?

Let's see, she thought. What is peace? A good feeling that everything's all right. And when does it come? When things are going well.

Then she saw it. Of course! God's peace came even when things weren't going well. It was still there when disaster struck, when your dreams fell apart, when you found yourself rushed off your feet the week before midterms, when you succumbed to midwinter blues. God's peace didn't depend on the circumstances. It depended on Him.

Kate closed her Bible and, a moment later, closed her eyes. The lamplight was shining yellow on the pages of her Bible, the voices of her parents came softly from the front of the house, the square of blackness outside her window was full of rain, the rain drummed against the roof, and all was well. It had been like this, this exact same scene, night after night for weeks, but it hadn't been beautiful until she had seen God in it.

The next day after school Betty Jane and Kate were standing on the porch, talking about the things that had happened during the day. Kate took a deep breath. It wasn't going to be easy to speak after being silent for so long.

"Want to see the poem I wrote yesterday?"

"Sure."

Kate handed it to Betty Jane. "I wrote it yesterday at your house, right after you said I was moody."

"Did I say that?"

Betty Jane read the poem. "It's beautiful," she said when she finished reading. She handed it back to Kate. "I really like it."

"You see," Kate said, "that's the way I've been feeling. You're right; I was moody. I let my moods get me down. But yesterday"—the words were tumbling out quickly now; she had to let them come that way or they might not come at all—"I found out that God is still there and I have to still keep following Him even if I don't feel like it. Then I know that He's still with me and I can still be happy in Him even when everything's falling down around me." She wanted to search Betty Jane's face for an answer, but she was suddenly too embarrassed. She looked away.

"I know what you mean," Betty Jane said slowly. "I always considered myself a Christian, but lately I've been trying to learn more about it and—take it more seriously, I guess. That's one of the first things I found out—that it's easier to be a Christian when everything's going my way, but that God's still there even when everything's against me. And if He hangs in there, I can too." There was a pause. "Anyway, I really don't know very much about it."

Kate was almost laughing. "You mean you've been discovering all these things too? Why didn't we ever share them with each other? I never thought you'd be interested."

"I guess I just didn't think I had anything to tell people that they didn't already know," Betty Jane replied. "I mean, I don't study the Bible all that much or anything, though I'm trying to get into it. But I've just been trying to get to know the Lord better."

"That's what I've been doing. I wish I'd known . . . now that we've told each other, can we talk about it together sometime?" She was suddenly shy with Betty Jane, as though they were strangers instead of old friends.

"I'd like that. I can use all the help I can get."

"So can I!" Kate laughed.

"Oh, no, you—"

"Hi, Kate. Hi, Betty Jane. What are you doing?" It was Andrea.

"Oh, just talking," Kate answered.

"About anything interesting?"

"Well, not really. Just things, you know." Maybe it was OK to share those "things" with Betty Jane now, but Kate definitely wasn't ready for Andrea.

Betty Jane surprised her. "We're talking about God. Pretty good subject, actually."

"Oh. Can I listen? People talk a lot about God in chapel and in class around here, but not that many people stand around talking about Him in the hall."

"Sorry if you think it's a weird subject," Kate said.

"No, I don't. It's just that my folks joined the church

about a year ago, and we hadn't been religious at all before that, so it's all kind of new to me. I guess at first I kind of didn't want anything to do with it, even after they sent me here, but now . . . I'd like to find out more about it, anyway. About God, and religion, and stuff like that."

"That's great!" Betty Jane said. "Being interested is the first step. We're just finding out a lot of things ourselves."

"Join the club, Andrea," Kate added. "I think I've come out of my state of shock now. I haven't talked to anybody about God ever since I started, um, getting to know Him—I was afraid people would think I was crazy. I didn't think anybody else thought that much about God."

"Sometimes," Betty Jane said thoughtfully, "I think that God is on most people's minds most of the time, only we never talk about Him. It's nice to have someone to talk to."

* * * * *

So I've learned the meaning of peace, Lord—Your peace, that stays when everything else is gone. And I've learned about patience—the thing that makes it possible to stay by You and appreciate Your peace even when things are getting tough. Thank You for giving me a joy that's not at all like the happiness of the world.

Thank You, too, for finally giving me the courage to share You with somebody else. I not only had the joy of sharing, but discovered that other people are finding out about You too. I'm not alone!

Now I won't be worrying about the highs and lows anymore. Things were exciting in the first few weeks of my Christian experience. Then life gets back to normal, life with its ups and downs. I know now that my relationship with You isn't an emotional high all the time—but it isn't something that disappears at the first sign of trouble, either. You're always there. Thanks for giving me the patience to stick by You. And thank You, Lord! Today the sun shone!

All my love,
Kate

SPRINGTIME
Being With Him

Dear God,   *April 16*

Spring is in the air! I'm almost sure of it, and I thank You. For me, before, springtime was always the time when I made exciting discoveries and figured things out. This year it seems to be the time when I'm growing closer to You. Thanks so much for giving me the opportunity.

* * * * *

"Thanks for letting me read it," Betty Jane said. "I'll have to show you one of my poems sometime."

"I didn't know you wrote poetry," Kate said with some surprise.

Betty Jane blushed. "I don't show it to a lot of people," she explained. "Anyway, until a few weeks ago, the only way I knew you wrote anything was by reading the poems you wrote in the school paper."

Kate was quiet for a minute. She had always thought she knew Betty Jane well, and now she was realizing that she'd only scratched the surface. Once a girl she knew had had a bitter argument with her best friend. The girl had told Kate, "I thought I knew her, I really did, but now I'm finding out that I didn't know her at all." Kate felt she could use much the same words to describe Betty Jane, but it was a different kind of knowing. She liked the things she was learning about Betty Jane.

The two girls were standing outside the school building, waiting for the ringing of the bell to call them back inside. As the cold weather receded, once again the parking lot and the school grounds were beginning to be dotted with students enjoying the fresh air and sunshine at lunchtime.

"What do you want to bet someone will suggest we have class outdoors today?" Kate said, laughing.

Betty Jane pulled her raincoat a little closer around her. "I don't think we're quite ready for that yet!"

"Remember Mr. Ames warning us that spring fever always comes early in senior year? I guess that's because we know we're going to be free not just for the summer, but forever!"

"At least we're not as bad as the juniors yet," Betty Jane said. "The day before yesterday, they had almost persuaded Mr. Hanson to let them have class outside when somebody suggested they should take a basketball along to help them concentrate!"

Kate laughed. "They really picked the wrong teacher to try that on."

"Oh, he's an old softie at heart."

"You think I don't know that? He finally gave up lecturing me on being late."

"I knew he'd have to give up sooner or later. Anyway, you're not late as much as you used to be."

"Temperance. Self-control," Kate replied with mock seriousness. "It's a result of getting my priorities straight. From now on, biology is the most important thing in my life!"

"That's too bad," said Jeff, who had come up behind them. "What's so funny, anyway?"

"We were talking about spring fever," Betty Jane explained. "What did you say was too bad?"

"Biology class. If Kate loves it so much, she should be in there." He glanced at his watch. "She should have been there about three minutes ago, actually."

"Oh, no!" The three seniors burst into the building and raced up the stairs. Jeff swung the door to the lab open and followed the girls in.

"Don't you kids hear the bells around here?" Mr. Hanson wanted to know. "We do ring them for a reason, you know."

"Mom gave me permission to have some of the kids in for dinner on Sabbath," Betty Jane told Kate after class. "Will you be able to make it?" she added as a worried look crossed Kate's face.

"Oh, sure. No problem." All the same, Kate was concerned. She'd been trying to avoid Sabbath afternoon activities with the rest of the group, trying to spend the Sabbath hours getting closer to God. She found when she went out with her friends that all too often the talk turned to subjects that weren't helping her to grow in Christ at all. The worst part, she knew, was that she found herself joining in those conversations all too easily—sometimes even starting them.

Don't be silly, Kate, she told herself. You can't hide yourself away from other people. Sabbath is a day for fellowship as well as worship.

But what, she wondered, is fellowship?

"Something wrong?" Betty Jane asked.

"No, nothing. What were you saying?" Kate decided not to share her concerns with Betty Jane just yet.

"I was trying to figure out whom I should invite. Jeff, of course, and that means Barry, too. I was thinking about asking Darleen Cummings. She goes to public school, her folks aren't Adventists, and she's new in town. I haven't really gotten to know her much, and I wish I had."

"Same here," Kate said. "Remember, she gave one of the testimonies at our visitors' Sabbath school."

"I'd forgotten about that. She comes every week, but no one seems to know her very well. Sue sits with her sometimes. Anyway, we'll ask her. Who else?"

"Andrea," Kate said quickly. "She'd enjoy it. And Terry Fields."

"In that case, let's ask Sue, too. She'll be good company for Darleen, and I think she and Terry like each other, don't they?"

Kate considered the idea and found that she didn't like it too much. "I don't think so," she said. "But ask Sue anyway."

"Well, that's seven plus me," Betty Jane said. "That's enough."

Alone again in the back bedroom Kate slipped to her knees. "Dear God—I want to use the Sabbath to be close to You. But I'm so afraid that I'll forget about You and I'll be no use to You or myself or anyone else. Please help me—I need You to be there and direct the conversation. I don't know, God. Just help me."

She leaned back and opened her eyes. Eight people, she thought, and I'm just one of them. Still, that means that one eighth of the conversation is in my hands. Can't I at least use my eighth to glorify God? If I can do that, maybe it will turn things around a little bit.

Sabbath morning after church Betty Jane rushed around the building trying to herd people together. When Kate finally arrived in the parking lot, Betty Jane had managed to fit Darleen, Sue, and Andrea into the already-full family car. There was no more room anywhere.

Betty Jane rolled down the window. "Barry and Jeff already left in Barry's car. They had some people to drop off."

"What should I do, walk?" Kate asked.

"No, Terry's back there trying to get his car started. You can go with him—he'll need somebody to help push."

"Thanks a lot!" Kate went back to where Terry was sitting in an ancient asthmatic vehicle. She got in just as the engine reluctantly coughed into life.

"I didn't know you had a . . . uh . . . a car," Kate commented.

"Not allowed to bring it to school," Terry answered as he struggled grimly with the gearshift.

"Aren't you too young for this kind of responsibility?" she teased.

"Watch it, senior," Terry warned, hauling the steering wheel around and directing the huge car out into the street. "I'm older than you are. I started school a year late. I'll be 18 in July."

"So will I . . . well, in August."

"It's nice of Betty Jane to have us in," Terry said. "What's the quickest way to her house?"

Kate directed him briefly. "Aren't you honored to have dinner with so many seniors?" she asked.

Terry laughed. "No comment on that. But I'm glad we're all getting together. I think it's good to spend Sabbath with other Christians—*as* Christians, if you know what I mean."

"I think I do," Kate answered.

Terry pulled the car up to the curb in front of Betty Jane's house.

Barry and Jeff hadn't yet arrived. The girls congregated in the bathroom to comb their hair, and Terry went into the kitchen to say Hello to Betty Jane's parents. Kate was left alone in the living room with Betty Jane.

"I really hope everything goes off OK," Betty Jane said, holding up her crossed fingers.

"Oh, it will," Kate assured her. "There'll be plenty of food to go around, even if Jeff and Barry do have fourth helpings."

"That wasn't quite what I meant."

"What did you mean?" Kate asked.

"Well, I think Darleen really likes to spend Sabbath with other people from the church, and it's nice for Andrea, too. I mean—I just want this to turn out to be a good Sabbath." She turned abruptly and looked at Kate. "After all, we all need it, don't we?"

The doorbell rang, but Jeff and Barry were inside before Betty Jane got down to open the door. "We're inviting ourselves in," Jeff announced. "Watch out for the invasion!" He kicked off his shoes and was, for once, ahead of Barry coming up the stairs. "By the way, Mrs. Donovan," he said, looking into the kitchen, "my folks asked me to ask you and Mr. Donovan over to the house later this afternoon."

"Oh, that'll be nice," Betty Jane's mother said. "I'm sure I'll be eager to get away from the noise by then."

"Mrs. Donovan!" Jeff said in a tone of reproof. "You know we never make any noise! You must have us mixed up with Betty Jane's other friends!" His dimples showed and his eyes sparkled.

After dinner had been eagerly devoured, the dishes had been washed, and Betty Jane's parents and little sister had left for the Wallaces' house, the guests sat around the living room talking. They got around to discussing the morning's Sabbath school program.

"I really liked it," Andrea offered, looking down at the piece of carpet she was twisting between her fingers. "I'm beginning to think Adventists aren't so weird after all."

Darleen laughed. She hadn't spoken much yet; she was a quiet girl who moved with a slight self-consciousness and seemed to be hiding behind her long straight hair. But she seemed eager to speak now.

"You're almost the exact opposite of me, Andrea," she said. "You're a non-Adventist in an Adventist family; I belong to the church, but my folks don't. But in a way we have a lot in common—so many things are new to both of us. Even after I first joined the church two years ago, I thought lots of things about Adventists were weird."

Betty Jane laughed. "I've been an Adventist all my life, and sometimes I still think that!"

Terry leaned forward in the rocking chair. "What do you think is weird, Andrea?"

Andrea looked nervous, as if she'd been backed into a corner. Her gray eyes shifted uneasily in her pale, pointed face. "Oh, nothing. It's just something I said. I didn't mean it." A pause. Then, "Well, there are so many rules and things that don't make sense."

Barry leaned toward her and adopted what Betty Jane called his "arguing position." "There are good reasons for all these rules, though," he began confidently.

"That's right," Kate piped up. To her own surprise, she heard her own voice, thin and silvery, cutting across Barry's warm golden one. "There are reasons. And the only really important reason is a relationship with Christ. The whole point of religion is to get to know Him. Then you have to decide whether the things you do are going to strengthen that friendship or weaken it."

"That's absolutely right," Terry said. Kate was relieved to hear him talking. She moved her hands, folded in her lap, so that her fingers were against her wrist, feeling her pulse. Would it ever stop racing?

Betty Jane, picking up where Terry had left off, started talking about her own Christian experience. Soon everyone was laughing. Betty Jane had the knack of telling a story in such a way that she was the butt of all the jokes, and her listeners found themselves laughing at her and turning around to discover that they were laughing along with her.

"So I just said, 'Lord, You don't need to worry about this one. I'll take care of this myself.' And I did. Afterward I wrote a story about the experience—I sent it to *Reader's Digest* as a 'Disaster in Real Life.' " Everybody laughed at Betty Jane's distraught expression. "For some strange reason, that's what usually happens when I give God a day off and run things myself."

Kate felt more relaxed. She was no longer nervous about her contribution to the conversation, and soon she found herself talking as eagerly as the others. Terry, Betty Jane, and Darleen were all sharing experiences and ideas. Sue and Jeff were listening quietly, and Andrea, though she seemed half bewildered, was smiling. Only Barry looked doubtful.

"Well, all this is OK," he said when there was a pause in the conversation. "But it doesn't really explain the rules. You have to have standards, certain very high standards."

"Yes," Kate agreed, "but those standards are a result of our relationship with Jesus."

"Sure," said Barry. "But that's such a vague thing. I mean, we have to pay attention to the practical side of things. The rules are still important."

Kate wasn't sure what to say. She hated to argue about such a subject, especially with Barry, who, she now remembered, always squirmed when a conversation began to take on a personal tone. It was Andrea, though, who answered him. "I think a relationship with God—like they've been talking about—well, it sounds pretty practical to me." She turned to Kate. "It's a whole different way of life, isn't it?"

"Sure is," Jeff said. It was the first time he'd spoken in a while. He followed up his words by standing up. "Why don't we continue this conversation somewhere else—like at the park?"

The suggestion turned out to be universally popular. Forty-five minutes later Kate was standing with her hands in her pockets saying, "There's got to be a log or a tree or something we can use to get across."

"Here's something," Barry called. He had wandered back from the riverbank where the others were standing, and was rummaging through the bushes. He emerged with a short, sturdy piece of wood.

"Armstrong, old buddy," Jeff said, putting his hand on Barry's shoulder, "I don't want to tell you this, but that little log isn't gonna make it across the big, wide river."

Barry gave him a withering look and slipped into one of his comic accents. "Well, old pal, the plan is this. See this big rock in the middle, here? We lays the log across the stream, and we rests it on the rock, and we walks over to the rock and jumps to the bank from there. Got it?"

Betty Jane was giggling at their antics. "I hope you've

enjoyed this presentation of the Armstrong-Wallace Comedy Hour," she announced, holding a tree branch like a microphone.

"Don't laugh, woman," Barry warned as the log dropped into place. "See what a masterpiece of engineering we have created for you? Come, I'll lead you across." He bowed in mock elegance, daring Betty Jane to be the first to cross.

One by one, the others followed. Miraculously, the log held. Kate followed Terry across. When he reached the rock, he held out his hand to help her across. In the middle of the log, Kate's foot slipped. She let go of Terry's hand and scrambled for a foothold. In confusion, she fell forward and landed hands and knees on the rock, Not until she heard a chorus of laughter did she realize that she was alone on the rock. Looking up, she saw Terry sitting in the stream a few feet away, staring at her incredulously.

"Well," he said, picking himself up. "Some people have all the luck."

Kate skipped onto the bank and Terry waded ashore. "You going to go back and change, Fields?" Barry asked.

Terry sadly surveyed his sodden suit pants. "No," he decided. "I think they'll dry out."

When the afternoon was over, they gathered back at the parking lot. "I'll drive Kate and Darleen home," Terry offered. "They're in my neighborhood."

"I think I'm actually closer to Barry's place," Kate said.

"Yeah, but he's got a carload. It's not far out of my way."

"Before we go," Betty Jane said, "I want to thank you all for coming over—and I wonder if we could have prayer to finish off our Sabbath afternoon?"

Barry stepped forward and organized everyone into a circle. Holding hands, they prayed together between the two cars in the parking lot.

Andrea came over to Kate and Betty Jane after they'd

finished praying. "Thanks so much—I had a great afternoon. My folks will be really glad when I tell them about it." She grinned quickly, and ran off to get into Barry's car.

* * * * *

I've discovered, Lord, that one of the best ways to get to know You better is to share my love for You with other people. Usually they have something to share too, and I get a whole new perspective on You. I'm so glad that I'm finally becoming more able to talk about my favorite subject—You! It sure is worth it.

Lord, You really are my favorite subject. It's so much easier to think or to talk about something else, but it's always worth it when I make the extra effort to keep my mind on You. And when I make the even bigger effort to orient my life around my love for You, the rewards are "exceeding abundantly above all" that I can ask or think! (I hope You don't mind my quoting from Your Book!)

All my love,
Kate

ONE LAST
PERFECT EVENING
A Question of Brotherhood

Dear God,   *May 25*

Why do You give such hard commands? "Love one another." Now that's a big one. Even if I could tone it down to "Be nice to one another," it would still be difficult. Of course, You said that, too. "Be ye kind one to another." Okay. It isn't easy. But like most of Your commands, it turns out to be worth having a try at. And I know that any real success I'll achieve will be only because of You working in me.

* * * * *

The door burst open, and Kate dashed through it. "I'm home!" she announced.

"And now the whole neighborhood knows about it," her father said. He gave her a kiss on the cheek. "Where have you been? Sit down and tell your old dad about it."

Kate poured herself a glass of milk before joining her father at the kitchen table. "I was at school, working on plans for the grad," she told him. "There's still so much to do. And we're running out of money."

"How much have you raised?"

"I don't know. It must have been a lot, though. We had two car washes, three bake sales, one movie, two craft sales, and no less than six cold-plate sales! When someone suggested serving cold plates at the graduation dinner, the vote was a unanimous No! We're so tired of them."

"So what do you have left to do?"

Kate rolled her eyes. "Only almost everything. We have to decorate the auditorium—and first, of course, we have to beg, borrow, or steal the decorations—and make sure the program is all lined up, and print our invitations and programs. Oh, and there's still the president's speech—Barry's been working on it for ages and he claims it still isn't 'exactly right,' whatever that means."

The whole class had been drawn into Barry's efforts to write his speech. They sat around the table at lunchtime and offered helpful suggestions.

"Make it funny," Betty Jane said. "Sort of off-the-cuff."

"No way," Nancy contradicted. "This is our graduation. It's a big event. There'll be teachers and parents and everyone there. Make it a professional job."

Barry put his head in his hands. "I think I'm giving up," he said. "Anybody want to be a last-minute president?"

Just then Bob came up and slid into a chair. He held a file folder in his hand. "Barry, old boy," he said confidently, "when you see what I hold in my hands your troubles will be over. No more speechwriting hassles."

"That sounds good," Barry agreed. He took the folder and glanced through it. "What is this?"

"The president's graduation speech—class of '74. There's not a soul here who'll remember it. I read it through—it's got everything. It'll be perfect."

"Oh, come off it!" Barry said and tossed the folder back to Bob. The others laughed.

"Whatsa matter? I thought you'd be grateful after I went to all this trouble for you."

The great speechwriting project continued.

"I don't know about the rest of you," Kate said to the group she was talking with at church the following Sabbath, "but we seniors sure could use a pre-exam, pre-grad break. Now that the weather's gotten warm, why don't we take a few cars, a few guitars, and something to eat and go out to the beach some Friday night. We could have a fire, and sit around and sing, and just relax."

"Sounds great," Barry said. "I nominate Kate Nichol to organize it."

"No way!" Kate protested. "I'm the one who needs the break, remember? Couldn't someone else take on the burden—some junior who doesn't have a grad to plan, for example?" She looked meaningfully at Terry.

"Or better yet," Terry said, "some college student who's home for the summer and doesn't have any exams coming up." He looked over at John Perry with a big grin.

"I think I could take over the responsibility," John said. "Everybody could bring something, and I can round up a few people to get transportation—shouldn't be any problem at all."

Kate broke away from the group as quickly as she could without being noticed and hurried to the ladies' room. There she stared into the mirror and brooded on the disappointment and anger that were vying for her attention.

"This should be fun," Betty Jane commented. She had followed Kate into the washroom and was combing her hair. "Looks like we'll be able to get the whole crowd out to the beach. One last bash for the year."

"I don't know if I'll even go now," Kate said with sudden fierceness.

Betty Jane looked at her with astonishment. "It was *your* idea!"

"*This* wasn't my idea. I should have looked more carefully at who was standing around before I spoke. I meant a nice quiet get-together, like we had at your house, with a few people that we can really have fun with. This is going to be a big free-for-all with all kinds of people coming—and John Perry in charge!"

"Oh, so that's it," Betty Jane said knowingly. "Do you still hold a grudge against him?"

"It's not a grudge," Kate insisted, regaining her composure. "It's just that the whole evening is going to have the John Perry seal of approval on it. Come to think of it, I probably won't even be invited!"

"Stop being silly. You can't have separate parties for the people Kate Nichol likes and the ones she doesn't like. Everybody deserves to have a good time at the beach, and everybody *will* have a good time. You'll have to leave your grudges at home."

Kate sat stubbornly straight through the sermon. She had done very well over the year with John Perry away at school. There was no need to think of the one person she really hated. Now he was home and intruding on what she had hoped would be a fun evening with her friends. She couldn't ignore him, yet she couldn't like him. In fact, she couldn't even bring herself to speak to him. She could picture her precious evening on the beach now: John Perry bringing not only his guitar but his unbearable arrogance, Nancy trailing along trying to attract his attention, Jean coming and making trouble—oh, she could see it all. A lovely Friday evening it would turn out to be!

She turned her attention to the speaker in hopes that the sermon would distract her from her thoughts.

"Christianity is easy on a desert island," Pastor Martin was saying. "Chastity would be easy if you'd never met a person of the opposite sex. Abstinence would be easy if you'd never heard of alcohol. Love is easy if there's no one around to hate." He leaned forward. "Christianity is easy until it's tested. But until it is tested, it isn't for real."

The minute the Sabbath dinner was cleared away, Kate excused herself and retreated to her room. Usually she looked forward to the hour after dinner when she was able to relax with her parents. But today she had a more pressing appointment.

"Christianity is easy until it's tested." The words drummed against her ears no matter how she tried to shut them out. Someone else might have found the test so easy that it would have been no test at all. But Kate Nichol, the one who talked about knowing Christ and loving people, the one who filled notebooks with letters to God, lay on her bed knotting her fingers together and silently crying, "No, Lord. I can't. I can't. It's too hard."

Never mind now that the hate she felt for John was all groundless, all the result of her own foolish mistakes. That didn't count. The hatred was still there, and how she acted toward the person she hated might tell her the truth about her Christianity—whether it was real or whether it was a game that she stopped playing whenever she wanted to.

All I have to do, she told herself, is to go to the beach next Friday night and treat John Perry and anyone who happens to come along with him just like I treat my closest friends, and to act as though all the people there are people I enjoy being with.

Put into words like that, it sounded possible, even easy. But when she tried to imagine herself at the beach, she knew it was impossible. She knew too that her old trick of ignoring John as if he weren't there was one she couldn't get away with this time. It was too easy—and it would make the party strained and miserable. No, she'd have to practice brotherly kindness—imagine treating John Perry as a brother! "Be ye kind one to another, tenderhearted, forgiving one another." She'd pinned Ephesians 4:32 to the wall above her bed, and now it was staring back at her, boldly daring her to take action.

She hadn't heard the phone ring, but she did hear her mother call, "Kate, it's for you."

"Coming," she responded. Betty Jane, leave me alone, she demanded silently. Anyone, no matter who it is, leave me alone.

"Hi, Kate? This is John."

This is unbelievable. This is not happening, she thought numbly.

"Hi, John."

"Kate, I know you're pretty busy right now but I wonder if you'd have time to give me a little help with the beach party. We're going to be out there past sundown, so we'll want to have a sundown worship. I wondered if maybe you could organize it—get someone to have prayer and give a little devotional talk yourself? If you're not too busy, that is."

"No . . . not really. I'm not too busy. But I don't know about giving a devotional. Couldn't you do a better job on that?"

"Well, I'm running the whole show," John explained.

Isn't that what you like doing—running the show? Kate thought. Instead she forced herself to say, "I guess I can handle it. I'd like to help."

"Well, that would be a big help. I'll call you Wednesday or Thursday to make sure everything's OK."

"Sure. No problem."

"Thanks a lot, Kate."

Kate hung up the phone, still not believing the whole scene. She almost laughed when she got back to her bedroom. "God, You sure have a talent for backing me into corners," she said. "Did I actually hear myself say I'd like to help John Perry? It couldn't have been me saying that, Lord. It must have been You."

The week went by all too quickly. For once Kate was sorry to see Friday roll around, in spite of the excitement of the rest of the group. She'd sent up a feeble prayer for rain, but the morning dawned bright, clear, and warm. Her case was hopeless.

Terry caught her in the hall at lunchtime. "I'll swing by to pick you up at around five-thirty, OK?"

"I'll be there," Kate said, trying to sound enthusiastic.

"There's something wrong, isn't there?"

"Sort of."

"Will talking about it make it better?"

She sighed. "No, talking about it will make it worse."

"Some problems are like that," Terry agreed.

"Anyway, I'm sure God can handle it for you."

Handle it for me, God! Kate begged silently. I know I can't handle it alone.

At five-thirty, squeezed into the car with Terry, Betty Jane, Jeff, Darleen, and Andrea, Kate still wasn't any surer about the evening. How could she give a sundown devotional at eight-thirty when by eight-thirty she might have failed miserably in the toughest task of her Christian life? She still didn't feel any inrush of kind feelings toward John Perry.

Coincidentally, John's car pulled up at the beach at the same moment Terry's did. They were the first to get there. Kate observed with a sinking heart that Nancy had indeed come along. It didn't look like she'd be fighting for John's attention, though—it seemed she'd already won the battle. Jean was there too, looking sullen.

Kate took a deep breath. Might as well plunge in with both feet. "Everything's OK for worship, John!" she called.

"Great! We've got two guitars here already, so the singing will go fine. You still leading out in the sing-along, Terry?"

Everybody suddenly became busy unloading the trunks. Kate saw Jean struggling with two cases of Vega-Links.

"Let me take one of those, Jean," she offered.

Jean grunted in relief and laid the cases down on the hood of John's car so that Kate could take one. "What are we going to roast them on?" Kate wondered aloud.

"I spent the whole afternoon untangling coat hangers. All my clothes are lying on the floor now," Jean said. She looked a little more cheerful.

Thank You, Lord, Kate thought. This one was easy, at least.

As Kate laid down the Vega-Links she saw John walking past in the direction of the woods.

"Want to come help me gather some firewood?" John

asked. He'd already recruited Nancy and Betty Jane.

Kate followed him. Glancing skyward, she murmured, "You don't let me off easy, do You?"

After several trips to and from the woods, John finally decided that the pile of firewood was big enough to last the evening. "Thanks for helping," he called as Kate made her escape.

"Any time," she returned.

"Don't say that," laughed John. "I'm going to need a lot more help before this evening's over."

The other cars had arrived by then, and the beach began to take on a definitely crowded look. Jeff dared Betty Jane and Kate to go wading in the still-chilly water, and they agreed to go—but only with his company. So the three peeled off their shoes and socks, rolled up their jeans, and stepped in gingerly, first one toe, then another. . . .

When they rejoined the main group, Kate noticed that Nancy had set up a card table and she and Jean were mixing fruit punch. "Wow, you guys thought of everything," Kate commented, walking over to them. "Need a hand?"

"All the hands we can get," Nancy said cheerfully.

"Looking forward to graduation?" Kate asked. Although she knew the answer, it was the only conversation-starter she could think of.

"You bet!" Nancy said.

"We've still got to get through finals first," Jean observed, staring glumly at the fruit punch.

"I may never even get as far as finals if I can't pass Mr. Ames's makeup tests," said Nancy. "I failed so many of them the first time around that I don't see how I can pass them now. Kate, do you think you could help me study for them?"

Kate thought of her own busy study schedule. But she would always find time to talk to Betty Jane on the phone or to kid around with Terry in the halls. Why couldn't there be time for Nancy? "I guess so," she replied. "I'll have lots of time to do it, so long as we get started early."

"Thanks a lot. I'll need all the help I can get."

The hours slid by, and in what seemed like no time Kate noticed that the sky was turning golden. "What time is it?" she asked Terry.

"Almost eight-thirty."

Kate looked up to see John approaching her. "It's about time for worship now, Kate," he told her. "I'll have the guys start up a song just to get everyone together and settled down; then you can take over."

"I'm nervous," she confided.

"Don't be," John assured her. "You'll do fine."

Darleen had prayer, and then Kate moved forward. She sat cross-legged on the sand in front of the group at first, but John motioned to her to stand up. "Hear better," he mouthed.

Kate stood. "I'm really glad everyone could be here tonight," she began. "I guess you all know that this is our last big get-together for the school year, and it means a lot to me especially, because I'm a senior and this is one of the last chances we'll all have to be together like this. However, as Jean pointed out to me tonight, before we seniors get our caps and gowns, we have to face a tough task—final exams. It seems like tough tasks crop up pretty often in life . . . "

Kate's voice got steadier as she talked, and she was comforted by the knowledge that nobody in the group knew that she was facing her toughest task of all that very night. She ended by reading a Bible promise of God's help and guidance. "Now," she finished, "Terry and John and the other guitarists are going to lead us in a real old-fashioned campfire sing-along." She sat down. "Did that last part sound corny?" she whispered to Betty Jane.

Betty Jane wrinkled her nose. "Well, maybe just a little." Then she gave her friend a broad smile. "The rest was just great, though."

Kate relaxed into the warmth of the fire, the darkness of the evening, and the fun of singing. She caught John's eye across the firelight, and they smiled at each other. With Betty Jane on one side and Terry on the other, Kate felt happy and secure. What a perfect evening, she thought, hugging her knees to her chest.

At around ten John caught her eye again. This time he pointed to his wristwatch. Kate was in charge of having closing prayer. This time she didn't bother to stand. "Since this has been an evening of fellowship and friendship," she said, "let's finish off with a prayer fellowship. Let's all divide off into groups of about four or five along the beach here and pray together, and when the last group is finished praying, we'll all join together and sing 'Side by Side' to close off the evening."

In the confusion of dividing up into prayer groups, Kate found herself separated from Betty Jane and the others. As she stood alone looking for them, she heard Nancy's voice. "Kate, we've only got three in our group. Want to come with us?"

So Kate knelt on the sand and closed off the evening by praying with her friends—one hand held tightly by John and the other by Jean.

* * * * *

I still don't know that much about love, God. But by trying to put it into practice, trying to be kind, I'm slowly learning. It isn't easy, and I'll probably have lots more "tough tasks" to face. But You can handle it for me, can't You?

I've learned the important formula that if I treat a person like a friend, I will begin to have more friendly feelings toward him. Perhaps even more important, I've discovered that my Christianity really does work when it's put to the test, but only because I let You take over.

I've got a lot to learn about loving people, Lord. Please keep teaching me. I don't always like Your

teaching methods, but I do appreciate the results.
Thank You!

All my love,
Kate

SENIOR SEASON
Charity *Is Not a Romantic Word*

Dear God,   *June 2*
Here I am, winding up the year. I wonder if I should have some kind of tally sheet to add it all up on—to see what it all comes out to. How far have I come? Sometimes I look at myself when I'm in a bad mood or I'm angry and say, "Kate, you're just the same person that you always were. Don't kid yourself that you're a Christian." But when I look at the whole picture, I know that things have changed drastically. And it's all because of You.

*   *   *   *   *

"Barry! Over here!"

The ball came curving toward Kate, but it was far above her head when it reached her. It landed firmly in Bob's hands, and he took off running. Kate sighed. Obviously she still wasn't the star of the basketball team.

A loud insistent clanging cut the action short. Mr. Hanson was standing in the parking lot ringing a large cowbell. He had adopted this practice in recent weeks, having decided that students had become deaf to the sound of the regular school bell. He had an added advantage this way—not only was his bell louder, but, being there in person, he could personally escort into the school building those students who still found it difficult to heed the call.

"We won!" Barry announced. "The seniors won the

last game of the year!" There was a triumphant chorus of cheers.

"Is it really the last game?" Betty Jane wanted to know.

"Sure," Barry replied. "Next week we have finals, and then it's graduation."

"I can't believe it." Betty Jane shook her head.

"I know what you're going to say," Kate said. "It went by so quickly. Seems like only yesterday we were excited about being seniors at last."

"That wasn't what I was going to say at all," Betty Jane contradicted. "What I can't believe is that graduation is less than two weeks away and we still aren't ready to decorate the auditorium and we still haven't decided where to order the cake from."

"You don't know a thing about nostalgia, do you, B.J.?"

They reached the biology lab on time for once. "Do you think Mr. Hanson will get softheaded because this is our last day and all and give us a free period?" Andrea asked.

"He's probably ready to die of relief 'cause it's the last day he'll have to put up with us," Betty Jane said.

Mr. Hanson was clearly less sentimental than most of his students. He felt that the seniors' last day at their dear old school should be spent reviewing for finals. By the time he had dragged them through an intensive review of the last six chapters in biology, Kate declared, "I feel more like checking into a rest home than marching down the aisle!"

Mr. Hanson heard Kate's voice. "Talking in class again, Kate? I thought I'd cured you of that. Would you like to tell the class what you were saying?"

Kate repeated her comment.

Mr. Hanson laughed and glanced at the clock on the wall. "Believe me, you'll be glad for all this hard work when you come to the final exam." He looked out at his class. "I've heard you all complaining at times that I've been too hard on you, and I want you to know before you go that I'm not sorry for it. The discipline I've tried to impose here is the same kind that you'll find out in the real world, where if you're five minutes late for a job interview you may not get the job. Life is at least as hard as biology, probably harder. So I have no regrets. But I do want you to know that you're one of the most enjoyable classes I have ever taught." The bell shrilled across the sound of his voice. "And I'll be very proud when I see you all graduate next Saturday evening," he finished quickly.

"That's right, man," Bob said as he passed the teacher's desk. "Give us the old soft soap right at the end so we'll love ya instead of hate ya when we're gone." Mr. Hanson looked at the boy and, with a smile playing at the corners of his mouth, asked, "Did it work?"

"Aw, sir, we would've loved ya anyway," Bob assured him, and made his exit amid much laughter.

The other teachers that afternoon were a little more relaxed when it came to giving last-minute work, but then none of them finished class with a word of praise, either. Mr. Ames did close off trigonometry by saying, "I wish I could say Goodbye to you kids here and now, but I've still got to get through graduation with you."

"It's obvious everyone loves us," Kate commented to Betty Jane as they left the building that afternoon.

"Oh, for sure," Betty Jane agreed ironically. "Look at all the fuss they made saying Goodbye to us. Even the juniors didn't wish us luck."

"Of course, they've got to show up to be our honor guard on graduation night. They'll probably get sentimental then."

Betty Jane's eyes twinkled. "I bet I know one junior who'll be sentimental when you graduate."

Kate ignored that. "I guess we have to come back Sunday to get the decorating started. We certainly won't have much time next week, and we can't leave everything till Friday. We have rehearsal and everything then.

This has been such a busy month!"

"Not so busy that Kate didn't find time to have three dates with Terry Fields!"

"Oh, don't be so silly," Kate said, tossing her head and trying to hide her burning cheeks.

"She's blushing, she's blushing! Hey, Andrea! Kate's blushing!"

Andrea, who had just come out of the school building, ran to catch up with them. "Why's Kate blushing?" she demanded.

"I only pointed out that she'd had three dates with Terry Fields in the past month."

"Hey, that's great!" Andrea exclaimed. "What's wrong with that?"

"Nothing," Kate replied. "Nothing at all. In fact, I think it's terrific. But there's no point getting all worked up over it. In the fall I'll go away to college and Terry'll be back here, so it's not as though it could be anything serious."

"Oh, anyone can wait for one year," Betty Jane assured her. "Then Terry will go away too, and you can be at college together."

"I hope so," Kate mused. Then she stopped short. "Listen to me! I must be crazy! Here I am planning two years ahead for a guy I've had only three dates with."

Betty Jane and Andrea laughed. "You can't help it," Andrea said. "That's love!"

"No," Kate was suddenly serious. "That's *not* love. That's wanting something for myself, wanting things to work out just right for me. Love is giving something to another person, and as far as that goes, I love Terry just the same way I love either of you, or any of the kids at school, or even John Perry. At least, that's the way love should be. I guess I let my emotions run away with me sometimes."

"That's natural," said Betty Jane, patting Kate's shoulder. "Some people are more lovable than others."

Andrea was not about to be diverted from the original

subject. "So, are you going to the grad banquet with Terry?"

"I don't know," Kate replied. "I guess not."

"Didn't you ask him?"

"I know it's my grad and everything," Kate said, "and I'm the one who's supposed to do the asking, but I just hate to do it. I get so nervous every time I think of it. I'll probably just go single like old B.J. here."

"Don't count on me," Betty Jane said with a small self-satisfied smile.

Kate turned around abruptly. "Explain yourself, Betty Jane Donovan!"

"Oh, it's nothing," Betty Jane said. "I'm only going with Jeff. It's not the same as a date."

"Aha!" Kate cried. "It's no wonder Jeff has that inferiority complex you're always talking about. Why isn't going out with Jeff the same as a date?"

"Well, I just figured that because our folks are such good friends, my mom had probably told Jeff's mom I didn't have a date, and she probably told Jeff to ask me."

"Betty Jane," Kate chided, "didn't it ever occur to you that Jeff might like you for yourself? You are pretty nice to him, and he probably appreciates it, even if you don't get excited about going to the grad with him."

Andrea was more eagle-eyed. "I wouldn't say she's not excited," she observed.

"All right, that's enough about dates." Betty Jane began to walk faster.

"Will Jenni Wilson be home in time for the grad?" Kate asked.

"Who's Jenni Wilson?" Andrea wanted to know.

"Barry's girlfriend," Betty Jane answered. "She's away at boarding academy, and Barry's going up for her graduation this weekend. Then she's driving back with him Sunday night. She'll be here in plenty of time for our grad."

"What's she like?" Andrea asked.

"Oh, like a tiny female version of Barry," Betty Jane

laughed. "Same blonde hair and big brown eyes."

"And that same ability to always do and say the right thing at the right time," Kate added.

On Sunday morning, Kate was at the school auditorium early. Betty Jane, Jeff, Andrea, and Nancy were also there. They waited outside until Mr. Ames appeared with the key.

"I want you to know," he said as he let them in, "that you really should all be home studying. Just remember that."

Nancy giggled. "We studied all Saturday night so we could spend today doing this."

"Not all day," Mr. Ames warned. "At noon I go home to make up exams, and you go home to study for them."

At ten o'clock, while Kate was standing on a chair pinning streamers to the ceiling, the doors burst open and five or six juniors strode in.

"We got tired of studying and came over to give you a hand," Sue announced.

Kate looked down quickly. Five heads below her, but none of them was the one she was looking for.

Sue saw her searching and said, "Terry's out in the car."

Kate felt the butterflies in her stomach fluttering. Whatever love is, she lectured herself, it is not thinking about your own feelings before somebody else's. All I'm worried about is how nervous I am. It never occurred to me to ask myself whether Terry would like to go to the grad.

Betty Jane was directing operations with a firm hand. "All right," she ordered, "we need someone to go out and get us some balloons. We forgot balloons."

"We don't need them now," somebody protested.

"We should have them, though," Betty Jane decided. "In case we don't have time to get them later." She had a dozen different orders for everybody, and two or three people decided that the best response was to take time out for their midmorning break. Kate, still hanging streamers, looked around to find herself alone in the auditorium.

Terry came in and surveyed the scene. "What can I do?" he asked.

Kate gave him a few brief directions.

"It's looking good," he commented. "Isn't it nice of us juniors to help you out like this when we don't even get to go to the dinner?"

"Well, you can go, you know."

"How's that?"

"Juniors can go if a senior asks them."

"Well, that's different," Terry said, focusing his attention on the cardboard letters he was hanging. "It's a little late for anybody to do any asking now."

"Is it really? That's too bad."

"Why?"

Kate took a deep breath. "Because I was going to ask you to come with me."

Terry climbed down off his chair and came over to where Kate was standing on hers. "And now you're not going to ask me?"

Kate tossed her head and turned her back. "The invitation's open, if you want to take it."

"Since you put it so nicely, I'd love to." Kate turned around slowly and saw Terry grinning at her.

"It's a date," she replied. The door opened, and Betty Jane and Andrea came in, their arms full of paper flowers.

"Perfect timing," Terry said, and went back to work.

Kate remembered hearing girls talking in the washroom last year about this time. "Any guy who's not in your class," one of them had said, "will be real nice to you right before your grad, just so he can get an invitation. It's not you they want to go out with at all—they just want a free meal."

Kate felt her throat tighten. Terry had been awfully nice to her lately—all of a sudden. I'll have to ask him, she decided. I'll have to find out somehow if it's really me he wants to go with, or whether he just wants to go to the graduation dinner.

She could imagine how hurt Terry would be by such a question, how he'd feel that he had to go out of his way to prove that he really liked her. The idea didn't make her feel too proud of herself, but Kate felt she just had to know what his reasons were for asking her out.

Terry drove her home at noon, after Mr. Ames had herded them all out of the building. They chatted about one thing and another as Terry's car chugged through the city streets, and Kate prepared herself to say, lightly, "Are you sure it's really because of my charm that you want to go to the grad with me? Or is it just the chance of getting a free evening's entertainment?" Something held her back from speaking, though. She decided she'd say it later.

Kate's mother greeted the news that Kate had a date for the grad with some amusement. "So, is this true love?" she asked.

Kate's answer was more serious than the question. "Mom, I'm not sure what true love is."

"Nobody's sure. What do you think it is?"

"True love—Christian love—is wanting to treat other people in the way that's best for them. Putting their feelings above your own, I guess."

"And romantic love isn't really much different," Mrs. Nichol replied.

"That's what I said to Betty Jane the other day," Kate answered. "But it doesn't seem to work out in practice. When I'm dating someone, I want the best for myself all the time."

Kate went to her room and pulled out her Bible. She began reading 1 Corinthians 13. "For about the hundredth time," she commented to herself. "I wish I didn't have to use a King James Bible, though. That dumb word *charity* keeps getting in the way. It sounds so old-fashioned, even though I know it's talking about love."

She went on reading, substituting *love* for *charity* every time she came across it. *Love* is almost a more confusing word than *charity*, she thought. It's all mixed up with the way I feel about Terry. When I say *love*, I'm never sure which kind I'm talking about.

With that dull, dutiful word *charity*, though, there couldn't be much doubt. That was definitely Christian love, giving love. Love that turned outward to the other person. Kate began to be a little glad for the old King James Version.

One thing's for sure, she thought. I can't accuse someone I have charity toward of being shallow enough to go out with me just so he could get to go to the graduation dinner. That would really be putting my own feelings first. Terry has always shown plenty of charity toward me, even when I didn't deserve it. It shouldn't be too difficult for me to show some now.

She went to the phone and dialed Betty Jane's number. "Betty Jane? Guess what?"

"You've got a date for the grad with Terry."

"Who told you?"

"Nobody. I'm a good guesser. So, is this true love?"
Kate smiled to herself. "You could say that."

* * * * *

At the beginning of the year, Lord, I thought of this as an experiment, something I could drop if it didn't work out. I thought I could still go back to my safe, cozy world where I took the truth for granted and never had to make any decisions about it.

Now I see, Lord, that once I've made a decision there's no turning back. If I ever moved away from You now, I guess it would have to be completely away. I couldn't go on imagining I was "safe" anymore. Now I know that there's no way to keep what I used to call religion in a box on the shelf. You have a way of moving into every corner of my life and changing things around.

When I was younger, I used to sit in church, in Sabbath school, in prayer meeting, and hear people say: "You can't be a Christian unless Christ is the most important thing in your life." And I knew for sure that that wasn't true in my life. But even up to the beginning of this year, Lord, I had myself fooled into thinking that there'd be plenty of time for it "later on." And at the end of every school year, or every summer, I'd look back and realize that "later on" still hadn't come.

It's come now, Lord. I know I'm still a long way from being a grown-up Christian, but I have at least come to the place where You are the most important thing in my life. I'm learning to turn to You first thing now, not only when there's trouble or joy to share, but also when I'm tempted to do wrong. It isn't easy, but I'm growing.

I was going through my papers from this year the other day and I found the piece of paper that Pastor Walters gave me that day in October when I went to see him. It says "2 Peter 1:5-7." I remember looking that up a long time ago and not really understanding it. Now I think I see.

"Add to your faith virtue." Faith came first, didn't it, Lord? Believing in You and accepting Your gift of salvation. I guess virtue is "being good": making those first attempts to do Your will. When I remember trying to do that, I remember how much it taught me, and I can understand why Peter says "to virtue, knowledge." Then there's that word "temperance." That always reminds me of the temperance booth and my horrible week before midterms. Then "patience"— waiting for You, going on serving You even when the circumstances aren't ideal. The patience that brings peace. It was after I understood that a little better that I began to grow even closer to You, to center my whole life on You. Is that what "godliness" means, Lord? I've always wondered. Being close to You led me into having to practice "brotherly kindness" and from there

You just continued teaching me about "charity." Isn't it funny that Peter uses that word too? I'm beginning to like it.

When I told Pastor Walters that I wanted a step-by-step how-to book, he told me that these verses were more of a description than a prescription. Well, they certainly read like a set of instructions, but I know I didn't set out to follow them step by step. Yet they do describe what happened to me. I guess the answer is that I didn't follow them, You did. But I tried to follow You, and that was the important thing.

So, Lord, there's no tally sheet. But I want to thank You with all my heart—and tell You that I'm looking forward to whatever comes next!

All my love,
Kate

EPILOGUE

"What time is it, Mom?"

"About five to seven."

"He's not coming, Mom."

"Calm down, Kate."

Kate twirled around once more in front of the full-length mirror. Her full white skirt billowed out prettily, but she stopped twirling. She was afraid her hair, carefully piled on top of her head for once, would come down.

I am now officially a high school graduate, she told herself. She looked again at the coveted diploma propped up on her bookshelf. Yesterday evening she had marched down the aisle behind Nancy, carefully watching her feet in hopes that she wouldn't fall out of step. She had sat stiffly next to the other girls, trying to keep her cap on. She had risen, trembling, to give the valedictorian's address and, moments later, been on her feet again to receive her diploma. The whole ceremony had been amazingly short.

Afterward the graduates had gone out for pizza to celebrate.

"You see," Jeff said, "this is what we should have planned to do all along. Just gone out together, had a good time, and not worried about having a big banquet."

"You won't say that tomorrow night," Betty Jane assured him.

Kate had had a busy Sunday. There had been endless

trips back and forth to the school to make sure that everything was in readiness, that the tables were set, that the food would be served on time, that every table would have a fresh carnation on it. Betty Jane still hadn't learned to drive, and while she could perfectly well walk to the school from her house, she seemed to have errands in every part of town that required transportation. Kate was again pressed into service as chauffeur.

At four-thirty they were driving down MacAllister Avenue with two boxes of white candles on the seat between them when Betty Jane let out a sudden "Oh, no!"

Kate, startled, applied the brakes. "What's wrong?" She heard a faint screech as the car behind her came to a stop, and another fainter one farther back.

"Oh, it's nothing," Betty Jane said. "Only I just noticed what time it is, that's all. I've still got to get a bath and do my hair and get my dress on and everything—I didn't realize it was this late."

Kate had seen Terry at least three times during the course of the day's activities. Each time he'd reminded her that he'd be picking her up at seven. Now, at three minutes to seven, she sat on her bed and told her mother, "He's not coming. I know he's not going to come."

The doorbell rang. "You see?" Mrs. Nichol said, going to answer it.

"It's the paperboy collecting his money," Kate called after her.

Terry was at the door with a white box in his hand. "I'm sorry," he told Kate, "but this is the only part of the evening I'm not looking forward to. I never did learn how to put a corsage on a girl's dress."

"Give it to my mom," Kate advised, and Mrs. Nichol pinned the red rose to Kate's dress.

"We'll be leaving in about ten minutes, Kate," her father called as Kate and Terry went through the door.

"That'll get us there in plenty of time, won't it?"

"Loads," Kate answered.

Terry and Kate were among the first to arrive at the school. Betty Jane, of course, was there, scurrying around giving last-minute instructions to the waitresses—sophomore and junior girls from the home ec class. The home ec teacher, who had offered to take charge of the meal, was anxiously trying to keep Betty Jane from getting underfoot.

Kate laughed and pulled her friend aside. "Everything looks terrific, Betty Jane," she said. "This is going to be perfect."

"I'm scared something's going to go wrong, but I guess if there was going to be a disaster it would have happened by now."

"Why not just relax and enjoy the party?" Kate suggested.

"I guess I'll do that," Betty Jane agreed. She sat down next to Mr. Ames and his wife and carried on a conversation with them for approximately a minute and a half. Then she jumped to her feet and excused herself to go check on something.

Kate watched the others come in. Andrea's date went straight over to talk to the other guys, and Andrea came to ask Kate to fix her corsage.

"I can't believe this year's almost over," Andrea said. "My parents are so happy that I lasted out my year at an Adventist school. They're going to be even happier when I tell them my summer plans."

"What plans?" Kate asked, struggling with the pink carnation.

"Oh, don't worry about that. I'll get my mom to fix it. I was talking to Pastor Martin last week, and he says I can take Bible studies this summer and maybe be baptized by the end of August. Won't that be nice?"

"Oh, Andrea, that'll be terrific! Haven't you told your folks yet?"

"No, I'm saving it for tonight. Kate," Andrea looked

straight into Kate's eyes and dropped her voice, "I have a lot to thank you for. If I hadn't been able to be friends with you and Betty Jane and the others, I would never really have gotten to know the Lord. I don't even know if I would have stayed here if I hadn't had friends like you."

Kate couldn't think of anything to say. She patted Andrea's shoulder a little awkwardly and finally said, "It's been great getting to know you, Andrea. I'm really glad for you."

Nancy entered, her usually straight hair a frothy mass of curls and her dress bubbly with lace and frills. She was clinging to the arm of John Perry—John, who, as usual, looked like a promising young executive.

Soon the room was full of graduates, parents, and teachers. Kate saw Barry and Jenni come in and went to welcome Jenni back home, since she hadn't had a chance to talk to her at the ceremony the night before and Jenni had had to miss the pizza party. Kate looked at the two of them as they walked away—Jenni petite and lovely, Barry tall and handsome. The perfect couple, she thought.

She felt a hand on her shoulder and glanced up at Terry. "Would madam care to be seated?" he asked with a formal bow. He led her over to the table where her parents were already seated. Kate looked over again at Jenni and Barry and realized once again that it wasn't necessary to be the perfect couple in order to be very, very happy.

The evening passed too quickly in a flurry of music, speeches, and laughter. When it was all over and most of the guests had gone, Kate and Terry stayed behind with the other graduates. Betty Jane busied herself clearing tables, but the others were sitting around laughing and reminiscing.

"Remember the time we tied Mr. Ames's door shut on April Fools' Day?" "Remember when we went on strike?" "Remember the chemistry test everyone failed?" "Remember the time Mr. Ames asked Bob if he'd read the algebra book and Bob said No, he was waiting to see the movie?" "Remember the cold-plate sale when Jeff bought zucchini instead of cucumber?" ("It all looks the same!" Jeff protested.) "Remember . . . ?" "Remember . . . ?" "Remember . . . ?"

I remember, Kate thought. How could I ever forget?

It was eleven o'clock when Mrs. Johnson and the home ec students appeared downstairs to announce that they had everything cleaned up and they were ready to lock the doors. Reluctantly the remaining graduates picked up their belongings and left the school.

Terry and Kate drove halfway home in comfortable silence. "I bet it's been quite a year for you, hasn't it?" Terry asked at last.

Kate leaned her head back against the headrest. "It sure has," she answered. "It's left me with a lot of memories, that's for sure."

"What's been the most important thing that's happened to you this year?"

Kate had no trouble answering that one. Tonight all her shyness and reluctance to speak seemed to be gone. "Getting to know the Lord," she said.

"Rats! I thought you were going to say going out with me," Terry laughed.

"That's a close second," she assured him. "But I never really knew God before this year, and God has definitely been the most important person in my life."

Terry was silent for a minute. "You don't know how good it is to hear that," he said at last. "I always knew from the things you said and did in public that you were a Christian, but you never seemed to want to talk about it in private, so I didn't know how important it was to you. I wanted to talk to you about it, but I wasn't sure you'd be comfortable if I did."

"Oh, Terry, it was never that I didn't want to talk. I was just scared to."

"Please don't be scared anymore. At least not with me. You can get so much more out of Christianity when you share it."

"I've been finding that out," Kate admitted. "And I don't think I'm going to be nearly so scared anymore."

They pulled up in front of Kate's house, and Terry walked her to the door. "Want to come in?" she asked. "My folks would probably like to see you."

"I'd like to, too," Terry said, "but I have to get home." He put his arms around her loosely. "Congratulations, graduate."

"It's so funny," Kate said. "It's my graduation night, and I'm supposed to feel sad because things are ending. Instead I feel happy—as though all kinds of things are just beginning."

"That's the way you're supposed to feel." Terry kissed her gently. "Every day."

Kate watched on the porch as Terry ran to his car. "I'll phone you tomorrow," he called as he got in.

Kate ran up the stairs and into the kitchen where her parents were waiting for her.

"So, was it the perfect evening?" her father asked.

Kate sat down and gave him a radiant smile. "Perfect in every way," she answered, and proceeded to relate every detail she could remember about the night.

A long time later, when the three of them were finally tired of talking, Kate found herself alone in bed in the back bedroom. Pictures of the evening, memories of the year, and plans for the future were all still buzzing around in her brain.

I still need someone to talk to, she thought.

Sitting up in bed, she switched on the lamp and reached under the bed for a 39-cent Bic pen and a ragged loose-leaf notebook. Opening the notebook on the bed, she began to write.

"Dear God, . . ."